The Pocket Guide to Scottish Place-Names

Alison Grant

Richard Drew Ltd
Glasgow

Published by
Richard Drew Ltd
Redyett
Balfron
Glasgow G63 0RP

A catalogue record for this book is available from the British Library

Editor: Iseabail MacLeod

ISBN 9781899471003

Typeset in Columbus

Layout: Mark Blackadder
Cover design: James W Murray

Printed and bound in China

Contents

Dr Alison Grant MA, Ph. D. is a graduate of the University of Glasgow, where she completed her Ph. D. on place-names and language contact. She is the Secretary of the Scottish Place-Name Society. She has worked for the Scottish Place-Name Survey based in the School of Scottish Studies at the University of Edinburgh, and is currently working as an editor with Scottish Language Dictionaries in Edinburgh.

Introduction

It is beyond the scope of such a small book to give more than a selection of Scottish place-names. Lack of space also limits the information provided on the names included to a very basic discussion of etymology, and a very limited provision of the historical forms which are so vital to their interpretation. For this reason, a list of suggested further reading has been provided, where more detailed information can be found, including useful internet sites and published sources including regional studies and classic texts such as W. J. Watson's *The Celtic Place-Names of Scotland* and W.F.H. Nicolaisen's *Scottish Place-Names.*

Arrangement of Entries

In the place-name lists, each place-name is followed by the modern local authority, and then one or more historical forms which help to illuminate the meaning. Historical forms are not provided for the more modern Scottish names, whose origins are well-documented elsewhere. The meaning of each name is then suggested, tentatively in some cases, together with the individual elements which make up the name. Where a specific element is given in a potentially unrecognisable (possessive, plural or lenited) form, the basic (nominative) form is provided in brackets afterwards, to allow for easy cross-referencing with the elements section. A pronunciation is also given for each name; it should be regarded only as a common modern pronunciation, rather than the only potential 'correct' one, with many names having differing local variants that are simply beyond the scope of this small book to record.

The Earliest Place-Names

The oldest surviving place-names in Scotland refer to natural features of the landscape, such as rivers and islands. Rivers including the Allan, Carron, Nairn, Naver and Tain and islands including Arran, Lewis, Rum, Skye and Uist are all likely to reflect a pre-Celtic Indo-European language. The lack of early records for this group of names makes it difficult to identify their origins with any degree of certainty.

Brittonic and Pictish Place-Names

The earliest Celtic languages in Scotland were Brittonic and Pictish. They were P-Celtic languages, representing a different branch of the Celtic family tree from Gaelic which is a Q-Celtic language. The P-Celtic languages were spoken across most of Britain prior to the Anglo-Saxon invasion of England in the fifth century and the expansion of Gaelic-speakers from Ireland into Scotland at around the same time. In England P-Celtic evolved into the Cornish and Welsh languages. In Scotland, P-Celtic began to decline in the ninth century and had probably disappeared altogether by the end of the twelfth century. The precise distinction between the Brittonic and Pictish languages is unclear, but the Brittonic language is believed to have been spoken in southern Scotland, and Pictish in the east and north. The two languages shared many common place-name elements, including *aber* 'river mouth' as in *Aberdeen* and *Aberfoyle* and *tref* 'farm, settlement' as in Tranent and Traquair. These elements are also found in Welsh place-names. Another common element was *caer* 'fort, stronghold' although this can be harder to spot because aside from occurring as *car* in names such as *Carfrae* and *Carluke* it is also disguised as *kirk* in names such as *Kirkcaldy* and *Kirkintilloch*.

Gaelic Place-Names

The Gaelic language originated in Ireland, and was brought to Scotland by immigrants to Argyll around the fifth century. From there the language spread across much of Scotland, and the presence of Gaelic is exemplified by place-names in *baile* 'farm, settlement' such as *Balerno, Ballantrae* and *Balintore*, and place-names in *achadh* 'field, secondary farm' such as *Achmore, Auchinleck* and *Auchintiber*. Another important element is *pett* 'land-holding, unit of land', found in names such as *Pitlochry, Pitmedden*, and *Pittenweem*. This was originally a Pictish element which was adopted by Gaelic speakers in eastern Scotland, and most of the surviving *pett* names appear to have been coined in Gaelic rather than Pictish.

A feature of Gaelic is the lenition or 'softening' of certain consonants depending on grammatical gender, number and case. This usually involves the addition of an *h* after the consonant in question, with names such as *Beinn Breac* becoming *Beinn Bhreac* and *Beinn Mòr* becoming *Beinn Mhòr*. This softening affects the pronunciation as well. For example, in Gaelic *bh* and *mh* are pronounced as English *v*, so that *Bhreac* is pronounced *vrechk* and *Mhòr* is pronounced *voar*. In some cases, Gaelic lenition is reflected in the anglicised spelling of names, such as Ben Vane, Ben Vorlich and Morven. The pronunciation of Gaelic names can be very difficult to reproduce orthographically, but a useful general rule is that the *ch* sound in words like *loch* is pronounced like German *Bach* or *ich* and not as English *lock*.

Old English Place-Names

The first Anglo-Saxon settlers spread into Scotland from the north of England during the sixth century. They spoke a dialect of Old English called Old Northumbrian. They settled in the Borders, the South-West and as far north as the Forth-Clyde isthmus. The Anglo-Saxon presence is characterised by place-names in *–ton* and *–ham*, such as Bonnington and Birgham. Their language was the ancestor of modern English, although it contained several letters which are no longer in use. These include **þ** 'thorn' and **ð** 'eth', both of which had a 'th' sound, and **æ** 'ash' which had a narrow 'a' sound. These letters were also used in Old Norse.

Old Norse Place-Names

The Scandinavians or 'Vikings' who first raided and then settled in coastal parts of Scotland from the late eighth century onwards spoke a language known as Old Norse, which bore a strong similarity to Old English. They established colonies in Shetland, Orkney and the Hebrides, and along the northern and western coasts of the mainland. There were also Scandinavian settlements in Dumfries & Galloway, the Lothians and Fife, although these may reflect secondary immigration from Scandinavian settlements in Northern England.

One of the most common Old Norse place-name elements is *bólstaðr* meaning 'dwelling, farmstead', yet it can be difficult to spot *bólstaðr* names, as they have evolved in a variety of different ways across Scotland. *Leurbost, Scrabster, Isbister, Risabus, Unapool, Skibo, Kirkapoll* and *Cadboll* are all likely to contain this element.

Scots Place-Names

The Scots language evolved in southern Scotland from Old English. Although the language had only a limited impact during the Anglo-Saxon period, in the aftermath of the Norman Conquest the Scottish royal family, most notably David I (1124–53), granted land to Normans who brought with them from England a retinue of followers who spoke a dialect of northern Middle English heavily influenced by the Scandinavian language. This Anglo-Danish dialect flourished in the burghs and monasteries, becoming distinct enough from the language south of the border to be termed 'Scottis' rather than 'Inglis'. The Scots language spread across northern and western parts of Scotland where it gradually displaced the Gaelic language, aside from peripheral regions such as the Western Isles where Gaelic is still spoken today.

Many Scots place-names are therefore quite similar to Old English and Old Norse names, with Scots *toun* closely resembling its Old English ancestor *tūn*, and Scots *kirk* closely resembling its Old Norse ancestor *kirkja*. For this reason it can be difficult to accurately identify the language of origin of some of these names, a task which is reliant largely on the geographical distribution of the names and the dating of their historical forms.

Place-Name Structure

Many place-names are formed from a generic and a specific element. The 'generic' element designates the function of place, e.g. town, hill, farm, wood, church, moor, stream, valley etc, and the 'specific' element defines or describes the generic in some way, e.g. small, big, white, black, narrow, cold, flat etc. The specific element can also denote possession, e.g. John's Town or Flemings' Farm. In the Celtic languages such as Gaelic, Brittonic and Pictish the generic element usually precedes the specific, e.g. *Baile Mòr* (literally 'farm big') whereas in the Germanic languages such as Old English, Old Norse and Scots, the specific normally precedes the generic, e.g. *Redkirk* or *Coldstream.* As the stress in place-names is usually on the qualifying element, most Celtic place-names have final stress, such as Dunbar (pronounced *dun-**bar***), whereas most

Germanic names have initial stress, such as Prestwick (pronounced ***prest**-wick*). There are however exceptions to this rule, with the Brittonic name Abercorn having initial stress, and the modern Scots name Clydebank having final stress.

Acknowledgements

I would like to thank those who were kind enough to comment on various drafts of the text, including Ian Fraser, Carole Hough, Simon Taylor and Doreen Waugh, and I am especially grateful to Iseabail Macleod for all her hard work in her role as editor. Naturally enough, any mistakes which remain are my own.

Alison Grant

Place-name Elements

a[1] from *Old Norse* **á** 'river' (Gisla, Laxa)
a[2], **ay, ey** from *Old Norse* **ey** 'island' (Jura, Stronsay)
aber *Brittonic/Pictish* 'river mouth, confluence' (Aberdeen, Aberfoyle)
abhainn *Gaelic* 'river' (Abhainn Bheag, Abhainn Ruadh)
ach, auch from *Gaelic* **achadh** 'field, secondary farm' (Achmelvich, Auchentoshan)
aird, ard from *Gaelic* **àird, àrd** 'height, promontory' or **àrd** 'high' (Airdrie, Ardnamurchan)
alt, ault from *Gaelic* **allt** 'burn, stream' (Altnaharra, Aultbea)
annat, annet from *Gaelic* **annaid** 'early church (or church land)' (Craigannet, Longannet)
aoineadh *Gaelic* 'steep promontory, sea cliff' (Aoineadh Fada, Fionn Aoineadh)
aonach *Gaelic* 'steep ridge' (Aonach Mòr, Aonach Eagach)
ard see **aird.**
arn from *Gaelic* **earrann** 'share, portion of land' (Arngask, Arnprior)
art see **ford**[2].
ary from *Gaelic* **airigh** 'shieling, summer pasture' also borrowed into *Old Norse* in the form **ǽrgi** (Fliuchary, Gearnsary)
auch see **ach.**
auchter from *Gaelic* **uachdar** 'summit, upper part' (Auchterarder, Auchtermuchty)
ault see **alt.**
ay see **a**[2].
ayre, ear from *Old Norse* **eyrr** 'shingle or rocky beach' (Earshader, Fugla Ayre)

bal from *Gaelic* **baile** 'farm, settlement' (Balerno, Balgowan)
balloch from *Gaelic* **bealach** 'mountain pass, gap, gorge' (Ballochmyle, Bealach nam Bo)
ban, bane from *Gaelic* **bàn** 'fair, pale, white, light' (Càrn Bàn, Tombane)
bar, barr from *Gaelic* or *Brittonic/Pictish* **bàrr** 'top, summit' (Barrhead, Barlinnie)
bea, beath from *Gaelic* **beithe** 'birch' (Aultbea, Cowdenbeath)
beck from *Old Norse* **bekkr** 'stream, burn' (Allerbeck, Archerbeck)
beg *Gaelic* **beag** 'small' (Cairnbeg, Drumbeg)
ben, bin from *Gaelic* **beinn** 'mountain' (Ben Nevis, Meikle Bin)
bie, by from *Old Norse* **bœr, býr** 'farm, settlement' (Duncansby, Lockerbie)
bister, bster, bost from *Old Norse* **bólstaðr** 'dwelling, farmstead' (Kirkabister, Scrabster, Shawbost)
blair from *Gaelic* **blàr** 'field, plain, cleared area' (Blair Atholl, Blairgowrie)
bo, boll, pool from either *Old Norse* **ból** or **bólstaðr** 'dwelling, farmstead' (Erriboll, Skibo, Unapool)
bodha, bogha *Gaelic* 'submerged rock, breaker' originally from *Old Norse* **bóði** (Bodha Ruadh, Bowmore)
bost see **bister.**
both *Gaelic* 'hut, church' (Bothkennar, Both Ruadh)
bowie, buie from *Gaelic* **buidhe** 'yellow' (Achiltibuie, Kilbowie)
bradan *Gaelic* 'salmon' (Clach a' Bhradain, Loch nam Bradan)
breck from *Gaelic* **breac** 'speckled' or 'trout' (Altnabreac, Breakachy)
bruach *Gaelic* 'bank' (Bruachbane, Tighnabruaich)
bster see **bister.**

buie see **bowie.**
bun *Gaelic* 'foot, base, (river) mouth' (Bunchrew, Bunessan)
burgh *Scots* 'town' or its ancestor *Old English* **burh** 'fortified place, stronghold' (Fraserburgh, Helensburgh)
by see **bie.**
caer *Brittonic/Pictish* 'fort, stronghold' (Carfrae, Kirkcaldy)
cairn, carn from *Gaelic* **càrn** 'heap of stones, rocky peak' (Cairngorm, Carntyne)
cambus from *Gaelic* **camas** 'bay, mooring, river bend' (Cambuskenneth, Cambuslang)
caple from *Gaelic* **capall** 'horse, mare' (Pitcaple, Portincaple)
carden, cardine from *Brittonic/Pictish* **carrden** 'thicket' (Kincardine, Pluscarden)
carrick from *Gaelic* **carraig** or *Brittonic/Pictish* **carreg** 'rock' (Carrick, Sròn na Carraige)
carse *Scots* 'low land along riverbank' (Carse of Bayhead, Carse of Gowrie)
clach *Gaelic* 'stone' (Clachnacuddin, Clachnaharry)
cladach *Gaelic* 'shore' (Cladach Chirceabost, Cladach Mòr)
clash from *Gaelic* **clais** 'ditch, hollow' (Clashindarroch, Clashmore)
cleit, clett *Gaelic* 'rock, cliff' originally from *Old Norse* **klettr** (Cleit Ruadh, Diraclett)
cleuch, cleugh *Scots* 'ravine' or its ancestor *Old English* **clōh** (Caldcleugh, Drycleuch)
clune, clunie from *Gaelic* **cluain** 'meadow' (Cluanie, Cluniemore)
corrie from *Gaelic* **coire** 'hollow in a hillside' (Corriecravie, Corrieshalloch)
craig from *Gaelic* **creag** 'rock, crag, cliff' (Creag Dubh, Duncraig)

crieff from *Gaelic* **craobh** 'tree' (Ballencrieff, Leac nan Craobh)

crom *Gaelic* 'crooked, bent' (Crombie, Cromdale)

cruach *Gaelic* 'stack, heap, hill' (Cruach Innse, Cruach nan Capull)

cul from *Gaelic* **cùil** 'nook, corner' or **cùl** 'back' (Culloden, Culzean)

dal[1], **dail, dol, dul** from *Gaelic* **dail** 'field, meadow, dale' (Dalmore, Dalnaspidal)

dal[2], **dol, dul** from *Brittonic/Pictish* **dol, dul** 'field, meadow, dale' (Dalkeith, Dull)

dale from *Old Norse* **dalr** or *Old English* **dæl** 'valley' (Clydesdale, Helmsdale)

damph, dav from *Gaelic* **damh** 'ox, stag' (Dava, Delnadamph)

darroch from *Gaelic* **darach** 'oak' (Clashindarroch, Knockdarroch)

dearg *Gaelic* 'red' (Allt Dearg, Beinn Dearg)

dhu, du from *Gaelic* **dubh** 'black' (Dullatur, Enochdhu)

doch from *Gaelic* **dabhach** 'land division, vat, tub' (Davoch, Dochfour)

dod *Scots* 'a bare hill with a rounded top' (Deuchrie Dod, Dod Hill)

dol see **dal**[1], **dal**[2].

draught, drochit from *Gaelic* **drochaid** 'bridge' (Frendraught, Kindrochit)

drum from *Gaelic* **druim** 'ridge' (Drumchapel, Drumnadrochit)

du see **dhu.**

dul see **dal**[1], **dal**[2].

dùn *Gaelic* 'fort, fortified place' (Dundee, Dunkeld)

dyke *Scots* 'wall' or its ancestor *Old English* **dīc** 'ditch, embankment' (Coatdyke, Dykeraw)

ear see **ayre.**

earrann see **arn.**

eccles from *Gaelic* **eaglais** or *Brittonic/Pictish* **eglēs** 'church' (Ecclefechan, Ecclesmachan)
eilean *Gaelic* 'island' (Eilean Donan, Eilean Mhunna)
ess from *Gaelic* **eas** 'waterfall' (Bunessan, Essich)
eun *Gaelic* 'bird, fowl' (Abhainn nan Eun, Loch nan Eun)
ey see **a²**.
eyrr see **ayre**.
fada *Gaelic* 'long' (Beinn Fhada, Loch Fada)
fas, fasadh *Gaelic* 'stance, stopping place, station' (Fasnakyle, Fassiefern)
fauld *Scots* 'fold, animal enclosure' or its ancestor *Old English* **fālod** (Langfauld, Stane Fauld)
fearn from *Gaelic* **feàrna** 'alder tree' (Drumfearn, Fearnbeg)
fell *Scots* 'hill, mountain' or its ancestor *Old Norse* **fjall** 'hill, mountain' (Criffel, Hart Fell)
fin, finn from *Gaelic* **fionn** 'white, light, pale' (Findochty, Fionn Loch)
firth *Scots* 'fjord, sea-loch' or its ancestor *Old Norse* **fjǫrðr** (Firth of Forth, Laxfirth)
ford¹ *Scots* 'crossing point on a river' or its ancestor *Old English* **fōrd** (Blackford, Redford)
ford², art, ort from *Old Norse* **fjǫrðr** 'fjord, sea-loch' (Knoydart, Laxford)
fraoch *Gaelic* 'heather' (Coire an Fhraoich, Freuchie)
gair, gare from *Gaelic* **geàrr** 'short' (Geàrr Aonach, Gairloch)
gart *Gaelic* '(corn)field, enclosed land' (Gartness, Gartsherrie)
garth from *Old Norse* **garðr** 'enclosure' (Applegarth, Housegarth)
garve from *Gaelic* **garbh** 'rough, coarse' (Garve, Garbh Bheinn)
geo from *Old Norse* **gjá** 'chasm, deep inlet, ravine' also borrowed into *Gaelic* as **geodha** 'chasm, deep inlet, ravine' (Geodha Dubh, Ler Geo)

gill from *Old Norse* **gil** 'ravine' (Capplesgill, Carlesgill)
glas *Gaelic* and *Brittonic/Pictish* 'grey, green' (Beinn Ghlas, Glasgow)
glen from *Gaelic* **gleann** 'narrow valley' (Glenfinnan, Glenmore)
gorm *Gaelic* 'blue' (Cairngorm, Meall Gorm)
gour from *Gaelic* **gobhar** 'goat' (Balgour, Meall nan Gobhar)
ha from *Old Norse* **hár** 'high, upper' (Ha Banks, Habost)
hām *Old English* 'homestead, village' (Birgham, Morham)
hamar, hamer, hamma from *Old Norse* **hamarr** 'rock, steep crag' (Hamera, Hamma Cletts)
hamna from *Old Norse* **höfn** 'harbour, haven' (Hamnafield, Hamnavoe)
haugh *Scots* 'a river meadow' or its ancestor *Old English* **halh, healh** 'corner, nook, river-bend' (Broadhaugh, Haughhead)
hest from *Old Norse* **hestr** 'horse' (Hestaval, Hestwall)
heugh *Scots* 'ridge, promontory' or its ancestor *Old English* **hōh** 'heel, projecting spur' (Corbie Heugh, Redheugh)
holm from *Old Norse* **holmr** or *Old English* **holm** 'islet' or 'water meadow' (Lady's Holm, Langholm)
hope¹ from *Old Norse* **hópr** 'landlocked bay, inlet' also borrowed into *Gaelic* as **òb** (Longhope, Oban)
hope² from *Old English* **hop** 'enclosed valley, hollow' (Dryhope, Hopehead Burn)
how, howe¹ from *Old Norse* **haugr** 'cairn, mound' (Hellihowe, Maeshowe)
how, howe² *Scots* 'a hollow, depression, low ground' or its ancestor *Old English* **hol** 'hollow, hole' (Howe Moss, Howgate)
inch from *Gaelic* **innis** 'island, raised meadow' (Inchaffray, Inchinnan)
inver from *Gaelic* **inbhir** 'river mouth, confluence' (Inverkeithing, Inverness)

kerry, kirrie from *Gaelic* **ceathramh** 'quarter, fourth part' (Kerry, Kirriemuir)

kil[1] from *Gaelic* **cill** 'church' (Kilbrennan, Kilpatrick)

kil[2], killie, from *Gaelic* **coille** 'wood' (Killichronan, Killiecrankie)

kin from *Gaelic* **ceann** 'head, headland, end' (Kincardine, Kingussie)

kirk *Scots* 'church' or its ancestor *Old Norse* **kirkja** 'church' (Falkirk, Kirkwall)

knap from *Gaelic* **cnap** 'hillock, lump' (Cnap Reamhar, Knapdale)

knock from *Gaelic* **cnoc** 'round hill, knoll' (Cnoc na Moine, Knockbain)

knowe *Scots* from *Old English* **cnoll** 'rounded hill-top' (Lang Knowe, Silverknowes)

kyle from *Gaelic* **caol** 'narrow' (Kyleakin, Kyle of Lochalsh)

lag *Gaelic* 'hollow' (Lag a' Choire, Lagg)

làirig *Gaelic* 'mountain pass' (Làirig Ghartain, Làirig Mhuice)

lanark from *Brittonic/Pictish* **lanerc** 'clearing, glade' (Barlanark, Lanark)

larg from *Gaelic* **learg** 'slope' (Largs, Largybeg)

law *Scots* 'rounded hill' or its ancestor *Old English* **hlāw** (Sidlaw, Traprain Law)

lax *Old Norse* 'salmon' (Laxa, Laxdale)

leck from *Gaelic* **leac** 'slab, flat stone' (Auchinleck, Leac a' Bhàinne)

len from *Gaelic* **lèana** 'damp meadow, green plain' (Lennie, Lenzie)

ler from *Old Norse* **leir** 'mud, clay' (Ler Geo, Lerwick)

letter from *Gaelic* **leitir** 'steep slope, hillside' (Letterewe, Letterfinlay)

liath *Gaelic* 'grey' (Craigleith, Monadh Liath)

lin from *Gaelic* **linn** 'pool, pond' or *Brittonic/Pictish* **llyn** 'lake' (Linlithgow, Loch Linnhe)

loan *Scots* 'grassy cattle track, leading to a grazing area' (Byres Loan, Loanhead)
loch *Gaelic* 'lake, sea-inlet' (Gairloch, Loch Ness)
lòn *Gaelic* 'marsh, meadow, pool' (Londubh, Lon na Cuilc)
lùb, lùib *Gaelic* 'bend, loop' (Buailnaluib, Lubcroy)
machair *Gaelic* 'fertile coastal plain' (Machrihanish, Machair Leathann)
maddy from *Gaelic* **madadh** 'dog, fox, wolf' (Ardmaddy, Lochmaddy)
màm *Gaelic* 'breast, rounded hill, pass' (Màm Mòr, Màm Sodhail)
maol *Gaelic* 'bald, bare round hill' (Càrn Maol, Creag nam Maol)
mara see **muir[2].**
mark from *Gaelic* **marc** 'horse, steed' (Glenmark, Markinch)
meall *Gaelic* 'round hill, lump' (Meall Dubh, Meall Garbh)
mey see **moy.**
mòine *Gaelic* 'peat, moss, moor' (Cnoc na Mòine, Mòine)
mol *Old Norse* 'shingle beach' also borrowed into *Gaelic* (Mol nam Muc, Rosamol)
monadh *Gaelic* 'mountain, moorland' (Monadh Liath, Monadh Ruadh)
more from *Gaelic* **mòr** 'large, great' (Balmore, Beinn Mhòr)
moss *Scots* 'boggy ground, peat moor' (Flanders Moss, Mossend)
moy, mey from *Gaelic* **magh** 'plain, field' (Mey, Moyness)
muck from *Gaelic* **muc** 'pig' (Culnamuck, Isle of Muck)
muir[1] *Scots* 'moor' or its ancestor *Old English* **mōr** (Muirton, Stenhousemuir)
muir[2], mara *Gaelic* 'sea' (Achnamara, Murlaggan)

múli *Old Norse* 'ridge, promontory' (Hartamul, Lianamul)

mullach *Gaelic* 'top, summit' (Mullach Buidhe, Mullach nan Coirean)

ness from *Old Norse* **nes** or *Old English* **næss** 'headland' (Bo'ness, Stromness)

neuk *Scots* 'corner, point of land' (Dykeneuk, Woodneuk)

odhar *Gaelic* 'pale, dun, tawny' (Meall Odhar, Odhar Mòr)

òrd *Gaelic* 'hammer, round hill' (Muir of Ord, Ord Hill)

ort see **ford²**.

pan *Brittonic/Pictish* 'valley, hollow' (Panbride, Panmore)

peel, pil from *Scots* **peel** 'tower, fortification' (Peel Glen, Pilrig)

peffer from *Brittonic/Pictish* **pevr** 'bright, beautiful' (Peffery, Strathpeffer)

pen from *Brittonic/Pictish* **penn** 'head, end' (Penicuik, Penpont)

pert *Brittonic/Pictish* 'copse, thicket, hedge' (Larbert, Perth)

pil see **peel.**

pirn, prim from *Brittonic/Pictish* **pren** 'tree' (Pirnie, Primside)

pit, pitt from *Gaelic* **pett** 'land-holding, unit of land', a loanword from *Pictish* (Pitlochry, Pittenweem)

pol from *Gaelic* **poll** 'pool, pit, hollow' (Polmadie, Polmont)

pool see **bo.**

pres, press from *Gaelic* **preas** 'shrub, bush, thicket' (Prescaulton, Tornampress)

prim see **pirn.**

quoy from *Old Norse* **kví** 'enclosure' (Beaquoy, Buckquoy)

rannoch from *Gaelic* **raineach** 'fern, bracken' (Kinloch Rannoch, Strathrannoch)

ràth *Gaelic* 'fort' (Ratho, Rattray)
ree from *Gaelic* **ruighe** 'slope, shieling ground' (Aultonree, Portree)
reoch, riach from *Gaelic* **riabhach** 'brindled, streaky, grey' (Alltreoch, Sròn Riabhach)
rig, rigg *Scots* 'ridge, high ground, narrow hill, strip of cultivated land' or its ancestors *Old Norse* **hryggr** and *Old English* **hrycg** (Mid Rig, Peelrig)
rinn from *Gaelic* **rinn** or *Brittonic/Pictish* **rhyn** 'point, promontory' (Rinn a' Chrubain, Rinns Point)
ross, rose from *Gaelic* **ros** '(wooded) promontory, point, woodland' (Culross, Rosemarkie)
roy from *Gaelic* **ruadh** 'red, brown' (Auchenroy, Sgòrr Ruadh)
rubha *Gaelic* 'headland, point' (Rhu, Rubha nan Gobhar)
sabhal *Gaelic* 'barn, granary' (Cnoc an t-Sabhail, Sabhal Mòr Ostaig)
sauch, saugh *Scots* 'willow' or its ancestor *Old English* **salh, sealh** (Sauchieburn, Saughton)
scall, skaill from *Old Norse* **skáli** 'hall, hut, shieling' (Langskaill, Scalloway)
sett, setter, shader from *Old Norse* **setr** 'dwelling' or **sætr** 'shieling' (Grimshader, Melsetter)
sgadan *Gaelic* 'herring' (Garscadden, Glac nan Sgadan)
sgòrr, sgùrr *Gaelic* 'pointed or steep hill' (An Sgùrr, Sgòrr Ruadh)
shader see **sett.**
shan from *Gaelic* **sean** 'old' (Shannochie, Shantullich)
shaw *Scots* or its ancestor *Old English* **sceaga** 'thicket, small wood' (Pollockshaws, Wishaw)
skaill see **scall.**
skerry from *Old Norse* **sker** 'sea rock' also borrowed into *Gaelic* as **sgeir** (Glas Sgeir, Skerryvore)

slew from *Gaelic* **sliabh** 'mountain, moorland' (Slewdonan, Slewmuck)

sloc *Gaelic* 'pit, hollow' (Slockavullin, Sloc na Mara)

spidal, spittal *Scots* '(mountain) hospice for travellers' also borrowed into *Gaelic* as **spideal** (Dalnaspidal, Spittalfield)

sta from *Old Norse* **staðir** 'dwelling, farm' (Gunnista, Wethersta)

stob *Gaelic* 'steep hill, peak, point' (Stob Dearg, Stob Dubh)

stour from *Old Norse* **stórr** 'big' (Papa Stour, Stour Houll)

strath from *Gaelic* **srath** 'broad valley' (Strathmore, Strathspey)

stron, strone from *Gaelic* **sròn** 'nose, point, promontory' (Strone Point, Strontian)

stru, struan from *Gaelic* **sruth** 'stream, current' (Sruth na Moile, Struan)

taigh, tigh *Gaelic* 'house' (Tighnabruaich, Tyndrum)

tarff from *Gaelic* **tarbh** 'bull' (Abertarff, Inchtarff)

tibber see **tober.**

tilly, tulloch, tully from *Gaelic* **tulach** 'knoll, hillock' (Kirkintilloch, Tillyfour)

tir, tyr from *Gaelic* **tìr** 'land' (Blantyre, Tiree)

tober, tibber from *Gaelic* **tobar, tiobar** 'well' (Tibbermore, Tobermory)

tod *Scots* 'fox' originally from *Old English* **todd** (Todhills, Todrig)

tom *Gaelic* 'knoll, rounded hill' (Tomatin, Tomintoul)

ton, toun *Scots* 'farm, settlement' or its ancestor *Old English* **tūn** 'village, farm, estate' (Grahamston, Laurieston)

tor, torr from Gaelic **tòrr** 'heap, mound, low hill' (An Tòrr, Torvean)

trae from *Gaelic* **tràigh** '(sandy) beach, shore' (Ballantrae, Tràigh Mhòr)

tref *Brittonic/Pictish* 'farm, settlement' (Menstrie, Niddrie)
tulloch, tully see **tilly.**
twatt, what from *Old Norse* **þveit** 'clearing, paddock' (Butterwhat, Stennestwatt)
val from *Old Norse* **fjall** 'hill, mountain' (Hartaval, Roineval)
vat from *Old Norse* **vatn** 'lake, water' (Loch Langavat, Virda Vatn)
voe, way from *Old Norse* **vágr** 'bay' (Scalloway, Sullom Voe)
weem from *Gaelic* **uaimh, uamh** 'cave' (Pittenweem, Wemyss)
what see **twatt.**
wick[1] from *Old English* **wīc** '(dairy) farm, settlement' (Hawick, Prestwick)
wick[2] from *Old Norse* **vík** 'bay' (Lerwick, Wick)
yett *Scots* 'gate, hill-pass' or its ancestor *Old English* **geat** (Kirk Yetholm, Whiteyett)

Place-names General

Aberchirder (Aberdeenshire) *Aberkerdour* c.1204 'mouth of the Chirder' from Pictish *aber* 'river mouth' and the stream name **C(h)irder* meaning 'dark water' from Gaelic *ciar* 'dark, brown' and *dobhar* 'water' which was probably adapted from an older Pictish name. The local name for the village is *Foggie* or *Foggieloan*. [*ab-er-**hurd**-er*]

Abercorn (West Lothian) *Aebbercurnig* c.731 'horned confluence' from Brittonic *aber* 'river mouth, confluence' and a Brittonic term related to Welsh *corniog* 'horned', a reference to the confluence of the Cornie and Midhope burns rather than a river mouth. [***ab**-er-corn*]

Abercrombie (Fife) *Abercrumbin* 1157–60 'mouth of the river Crombie' from Pictish *aber* 'river mouth' and river-name *Crombie* meaning 'winding (river)' from Gaelic *crombadh* 'bending, winding', which probably replaces an earlier Pictish cognate form. [*ab-er-**crom**-bee*]

Aberdeen (Aberdeenshire) *Aberdon* 1172, *Aberden* c.1180 'mouth of the river Don' from Pictish *aber* 'river mouth' and the name of the Celtic river goddess *Devona*. [*ab-er-**deen***]

Aberdour (Fife) *Abirdoure* 1179 'mouth of the Dour' from Pictish *aber* 'river mouth' and the Dour Burn. The burn name is from *duvr*, a Pictish word for water, which was later Gaelicised as *dobhar*. [*ab-er-**dowr***]

Aberfeldy (Perth & Kinross) *Abrefrally* 1526, *Abirfeldy* 1552 'mouth of the Peallaidh' from Pictish *aber* 'river mouth' and a river-name which may include the name of the legendary water sprite *Peallaidh*, whose name means 'shaggy' in Gaelic. [*ab-er-**fell**-dee*]

Aberfoyle (Stirling) *Abirfull* 1481 'confluence of the sluggish stream' from Brittonic/Pictish *aber* 'river mouth' and either Gaelic *poll* 'pool, sluggish water' or more probably Brittonic/Pictish **pol* with the same meaning. [*ab-er-**foil***]

Aberlady (East Lothian) *Aberlauedy* c.1221 'rotten river mouth' from Brittonic *aber* 'river mouth' and a lost Brittonic word which was cognate with Gaelic *lobh* 'rot, putrify'. The second element may originally have been a river-name. [*ab-er-**lay**-dee*]

Aberlour (Moray) *Aberlower* 1226 'confleunce of the Lour burn' from Pictish *aber* 'river mouth, confluence' and the Lour Burn, derived from Gaelic *labhar* 'loud, noisy', probably replacing a Pictish cognate form. The burn meets the River Spey at Aberlour. The current name of **Charlestown of Aberlour** reflects nineteenth-century redevelopment by Charles Grant of Elchies. [*ab-er-**lowr***]

Abernethy (Perth & Kinross) *Aburnethige* 10thC 'mouth of the river Nethy' from Pictish *aber* 'river mouth' and the river-name *Nethy*, which is from a Celtic root *nect-*, meaning 'pure, clear'. [*ab-er-**neth**-ee*]

Achmore (Highland, Western Isles) *Achmoir* 1495 (H) 'big field' Gaelic *achadh* 'field' and *mòr* 'big, great' [*ach-**moar***]

Achnahannet (Highland) *Auchnahannatt* 1589 'field of the mother church' from Gaelic *achadh* 'field' *na h-* 'of the' *annaid* 'mother church, early church'. [ach-na-**ha**-nit]

Achnamara (Argyll & Bute) *Achnamara* 1755 'field by the sea' from Gaelic *achadh* 'field' *na* 'by the' *mara* (from *muir*) 'sea'. [*ach-na-**mar**-a*]

Achnashellach (Highland) *Auchinsellach* 1584 'field of the willows' from Gaelic *achadh* 'field' *nan* 'of the' *seilich* (from *seileach*) 'willows'. [*ach-na-**shell**-ach*]

Affleck (Aberdeenshire) *Auhelic* 1200–14, *Auchlek* 1493 'slab field' from Gaelic *achadh* 'field' and *leac* 'slab, flagstone'. Compare **Auchinleck**. [*aff-lick*, locally *aff-**leck***]

Airdrie (North Lanarkshire) *Ardrie* 1587 'high slope' from Gaelic *àrd* 'high' and *ruighe* 'slope, shieling ground'. [***air**-dree*]

Aith (Shetland) *Aith* 1578 'isthmus' from Old Norse *eið* 'isthmus'. [***aid***]

Alexandria (West Dunbartonshire) An eighteenth-century name commemorating local landowner and MP, Alexander Smollett. [*ah-leg-**zan**-dree-a*]

Allerbeck (Dumfries & Galloway) *Elrebec* c.1218 'burn of the alder trees' from Old Norse *elri* 'alder trees' and *bekkr* 'stream, burn'. [***al**-er-beck*]

Alloa (Clackmannanshire) *Auleway* 1364 'rocky plain' from the old Gaelic compound *allmhagh* derived from the elements *ail* 'rock, stone' and *magh* 'plain, field'. [***al**-oh-a*]

Alloway (South Ayrshire) *Auleway* 1324 like Alloa above, this means 'rocky plain' from the old Gaelic compound *allmhagh* derived from the elements *ail* 'rock, stone' and *magh* 'plain, field'. [***al**-oh-way*]

Alness (Highland) *Alenes* 1227 possibly 'place on the Allan' from the pre-Celtic river name **Alauna* meaning 'the flowing one' and Gaelic *fas* 'station, place, level spot', or alternatively it may be an Old Norse name containing *nes* 'headland' as the second element. [***ol**-ness*, locally ***al**-ness*]

Altnaharra (Highland) *Aldnahervie* 1755 'stream at the boundary wall' from Gaelic *allt* 'burn, stream' *na h-* 'of the' *airbhe, eirbhe* 'dividing wall, boundary'. [*alt-na-**har**-a*]

Alva (Clackmannanshire) *Alveth* 1357 'rocky plain' from the old Gaelic compound *allmhagh* derived from the elements *ail* 'rock, stone' and *magh* 'plain, field', like Alloa above. [***al**-va*]

Annan (Dumfries & Galloway) *Estrahanent* 1124, *Stratanant* 1152 '(place by) the river Annan'. The river may be named after the Goddess *Anu.* The earliest form contains Brittonic *ystrad,* cognate with Gaelic *srath* 'broad valley'. A later form *Anandredalle* c.1360 (modern Annandale) reveals that *ystrad* was replaced by Old Norse *dalr* with the same meaning. [***an**-an*]

Anstruther (Fife) *Ainestroder* 1178–88, *Eynstrother* 1243 perhaps 'driving burn' or '(place of) one burn' from either Gaelic *á(i)n* 'driving' or *aon* 'one' and *sruthair* 'burn, current'. [***an**-struth-er,* locally ***en**-ster*]

Applecross (Highland) *Aporcrosan* 673, *Ablecross* 1275 'mouth of the river Crosan' from Pictish *aber* 'river mouth' and the Gaelic river-name *Crosan* 'little cross' from *crois* 'cross' with the diminutive suffix *–an.* This has been anglicised to *Applecross,* and the modern Gaelic name is *A' Chomraich* 'the sanctuary'. [***ap**-il-cross*]

Applegarth (Dumfries & Galloway) *Apilgirth* 1275, *Apilgarth* 1361 '(enclosed) apple orchard' from the Old Norse compound *apaldr(s)-garth* 'apple-orchard' from *apaldr* 'apple-tree' and *garðr* 'enclosure'. [***ap**-il-girth*]

Arbroath (Angus) *Aberbrudoc* 1189–98, *Abirbrothoc* 1199 'mouth of the Brothock burn' from Pictish *aber* 'river-mouth' and the Brothock Burn. The name of the burn is from Gaelic *brothach* 'boiling, seething', although this probably replaces an earlier Pictish form. [*ar-**broath***]

Ardentinny (Argyll & Bute) *Ardintinie* 1750 'headland of the fox' from Gaelic *àird, àrd* 'height, promontory' *an t-* 'of the' and *sionnaich* (from *sionnach*) 'fox'. [*ard-in-**tin**-ee*]

Ardersier (Highland) *Ardrosser* 1227 In modern Gaelic 'headland of the carpenters' from Gaelic *àird, àrd* 'height, promontory' *nan* 'of the' *saoir* (from *saor*) 'carpenter'. However the historical form reveals that the name may originally have meant 'height of Rosser' from an existing place-name **Rosser*, containing Gaelic or Pictish *ros* 'point, promontory'. [*ard-er-**seer***]

Ardgay (Highland) *Ardgy* 1627, *Ardgye* 1642 'windy promontory' from Gaelic *àird, àrd* 'height, promontory' and *ghaoithe* (from *gaoth*) 'wind'. [*ard-**guy***]

Ardgour (Highland) *Ardegoware* 1371–72 'goat promontory' from Gaelic *àird, àrd* 'height, promontory' and *gobhar* 'goat'. [*ard-**gowr***]

Ardhallow (Argyll & Bute) *Ardhallowane* 1545 'high land' from Gaelic *àrd* 'high' and *talamh* 'land'. [*ard-**hal**-oh*]

Ardnamurchan (Highland) *Art Murchol* c. 700 'promontory of the otters' from Gaelic *àird, àrd* 'height, promontory' *nam* 'of the' *murchan* (from *muirchù*) 'otters, sea-hounds', although the early form suggests that the original final element was *muirchol* 'sea-wickedness, piracy'. [*ard-na-**murch**-an*]

Ardrossan (North Ayrshire) *Ardrossane* 1315–21 perhaps 'height of the little promontory' from Gaelic *àird, àrd* 'height, promontory' *ros* 'point, promontory' and the diminutive suffix *–an* 'little'. [*ar-**dross**-an*]

Argyll (Argyll & Bute) *Arregaithel* c.970, *Argail* 1292 'coastland of the Gaels' from Gaelic *oirthir* 'coast, shore' and *Ghàidheal* (from *Gàidheal*) 'Gael, Gaelic-speaker'. [*ar-**gyle***]

Armadale (Highland, West Lothian) *Armidill* 1499 (H) 'arm-shaped valley' from Old Norse *armr* 'arm' and *dalr* 'valley'. The West Lothian name is a transplant from Sutherland. [***arm**-ah-dail*]

Arnprior (Stirling) *Arnepriour* 1584, *Arnpryer* 1750 'the prior's portion of land' from Gaelic *earrann* 'share, portion of land' and probably Scots or Latin *prior* 'monastic superior', although the word may also have been borrowed into Gaelic. [*arn-**pry**-or*]

Arran (North Ayshire) *Aran* c.1294, *Arane* 1364 This name is obscure. A common explanation is 'kidney-shaped isle' from Early Gaelic *aru* 'kidney', but the name is likely to belong to the earlier pre-Celtic period. [***ar**-an*]

Auchinleck (East Ayrshire) *Achinlek* 1392–93 'field of the flat stones' from Gaelic *achadh* 'field' *nan* 'of the' *leac* 'slabs, flagstones'. Compare **Affleck.** [*och-in-**leck***]

Auchintiber (North Ayrshire) *Auchinteber* 1535 'field of the well' from Gaelic *achadh* 'field' *an* 'of the' *tobair* (from *tobar*) 'well'. [*och-in-**tee**-ber*]

Auchterarder (Perth & Kinross) *Uchtirardour* 1327–28 'upland of the high water' from Gaelic *uachdar* 'summit, upper part' *àrd* 'high' and *dobhar* 'water'. [*och-ter-**ard**-er*]

Auchterderran (Fife) *Hurkyndorath* c.1053–93, *Ochtirdere* 1400 The original first element is obscure, but by the fifteenth century it had been assimilated to Gaelic *uachdar* 'summit, upper part'. The second element may have been Gaelic *deòradh* 'dewar' (relic-keeper). [*och-ter-**der**-an*]

Auchterless (Aberdeenshire) *Uchtirlys* 1211–14, *Ochterlys* 1358 'upland of the enclosure' from Gaelic *uachdar* 'summit, upper part' and *lios* 'garden, enclosure'. [och-ter-**less**]

Auchtermuchty (Fife) *Uchtermukethin* 1205–11, *Vctermokethin* 1244 'upland of the swine place' from Gaelic *uachdar* 'summit, upper part' and *muic* (from *muc*) 'pigs, swine' followed by *atu/etu* and *–in*, combining to mean 'place of'. [*och-ter-**much**-tay*]

Auchtertool (Fife) *Outhertule* 1132–53, *Ochtirtule* c.1229–36 'upland of the Tiel (burn)' from Gaelic *uachdar* 'summit, upper part' and the burn name *Tiel*, which derives from *tuil* 'flood'. [*och-ter-**tool***]

Aultbea (Highland) from Gaelic *allt* 'burn, stream' and *beithe* 'birch'. [*olt-**bay***]

Aviemore (Highland) *Avymoir* 1654 'the big hill-face' from Gaelic *aghaidh* 'face' and *mòr* 'big, great'. [*av-ee-**moar***]

Avoch (Highland) *Auach* 1328 'river place' from Gaelic *abh* 'river, stream', with an *–ach* suffix indicating 'place of'. [***och***]

Ayr (South Ayrshire) *Inber-air* 1490 'mouth of the River Ayr'. Known simply as *Ayr* in modern times, it was previously called *Inbhir-àir*, from Gaelic *inbhir* 'river mouth, confluence' and a possibly Celtic river name from the root **Arā* meaning 'water-course, river'. [***air***]

Balbarton (Fife) *Balbretanis* 1369 'farm of the Briton(s)' from Gaelic *baile* 'farm, settlement' and *Breatan* 'Briton'. [*bal-**bar**-tin*]

Balerno (Edinburgh) *Balhernoch* 1280, *Balernauch* 1283 'farm of the sloe-tree' from Gaelic *baile* 'farm, settlement' and *airneach* 'sloe-tree'. [*ba-**ler**-no*]

Balfron (Stirling) *Buthbren* 1233 This name has been explained as containing Gaelic *baile* 'farm, settlement' and a personal name derived from *freòine* 'fury, rage', in parallel with the River Fruin near Loch Lomond. However, the earliest form suggests instead Gaelic *both* 'hut, church' and perhaps the name of a saint. [*bal-**fron***]

Balgowan (Dumfries & Galloway, Perth & Kinross) *Ballingowin* 1467 (DG), *Balgowny* 1535 (PK) 'farm of the smith' from Gaelic *baile* 'farm, settlement' and *gobhainn* (from *gobha*) 'blacksmith'. [*bal-**gow**-an*]

Balintore (Highland, Angus) *Balindar* 1662, *Balindor* 1750 (H) 'farm of the bleaching' from Gaelic *baile* 'farm, settlement' *an* 'of the' *todhair* (from *todhar*) 'bleach, manure, manured field'. [*bal-in-**toar***]

Ballachulish (Highland) *Balcholish* 1750 'settlement of the strait' from Gaelic *baile* 'farm, settlement' *an* 'of the' *caolais* (from *caolas*) 'strait, sound'. [*ba-la-**hool**-ish*]

Ballantrae (South Ayrshire) *Ballentray* 1541 'farm on the shore' from Gaelic *baile* 'farm, settlement' *an* 'of the' *tràighe* (from *tràigh*) 'beach, shore'. [*bal-an-**tray***]

Ballater (Aberdeenshire) *Balader* 1704, *Ballader* 1716 This name is obscure, and the initial stress suggests that it is unlikely to be a *baile* name. [***bal**-a-ter*]

Ballencrieff (East Lothian, West Lothian) *Balnecref* 1335–36 (WL), *Ballincreif* 1515 (EL) 'farm by the tree' from Gaelic *baile* 'farm, settlement' *na* 'of the' *craoibhe* (from *craobh*) 'tree'. [*bal-in-**kreef***]

Ballinluig (Perth & Kinross) *Balinluig* 1750 'farm at the hollow' from Gaelic *baile* 'farm, settlement' *an* 'at the' *luig* (from *lag*) 'hollow'. [*bal-in-**loo**-ig*]

Balloch (West Dunbartonshire) *Bellach* 1238 'mountain pass' from Gaelic *bealach* 'mountain pass, gap, gorge'. [***bal**-och*] Balloch near Inverness is 'lake farm' from Gaelic *baile* 'farm, settlement' and *loch* 'lake, sea-inlet'. [*ba-**loch***]

Ballygown (Argyll & Bute) *Balligoun* 1820 'farm of the smith' from Gaelic *baile* 'farm, settlement' a''of the' *gobhainn* (from *gobha*) 'blacksmith'. [*bal-ee-**gown***]

Balmaclennan (Dumfries & Galloway) *Balmaclenan* 1453 'Maclennan's farm' from Gaelic *baile* 'farm, settlement' and the surname Maclennan. [*bal-ma-**klen**-an*]

Balnahard (Argyll & Bute) *Balnahard* 1750 (Mull), *Balnaard* 1750 (Colonsay) 'farm at the promontory' from Gaelic *baile* 'farm, settlement' *na h-* 'of the' *àirde* (from *àird*) 'height, promontory'. [*bal-na-**hard***]

Balnakyle (Highland) 'farm at the wood' from Gaelic *baile* 'farm, settlement' *na* 'of the' *coille* 'wood'. [*bal-na-**kyle***]

Banchory (Aberdeenshire) *Benchoryn* 1203–14, *Banquhory* 1472 perhaps 'horn-shaped place' from Gaelic *beannchar* 'horn-cast', referring to a horn-like river-bend. [***ban**-kor-ee*]

Banff (Aberdeenshire) *Banb* c.1150 either from Gaelic *banba* 'Ireland' as a name imported by Irish settlers to the area, or from Gaelic *banbh* 'piglet' as an animal term applied to the River Deveron. [***bamf*, *banf***]

Bannockburn (Stirling) *Bannock burne* 1654 'the burn at the peaked place' from Brittonic *bannauc* 'peaked, horned' to which Scots *burn* 'stream' was latter added. [***ban**-ock-burn*]

Bantaskin (Stirling) *Pettintoscale* 1450, *Pantaskane* 1640 'the land-holding of the gospel' from Gaelic *pett* 'land-holding, unit of land' *an t-* 'of the' *soisgeil* 'gospel'. The land may have been gifted to the church. [*ban-**task**-in*]

Bathgate (West Lothian) *Batket* 1153–65 'boar wood' from Brittonic *baedd* 'boar' and **cēt* 'wood'. [***bath**-gait*]

Beauly (Highland) *Bewlie* 1655, *Beauly* 1764 'beautiful place' from French *beau* 'beautiful' and *lieu* 'place'. [***byoo**-lee*]

Beith (North Ayrshire) *Beith* 1544 'place of birch trees' from Gaelic *beithe* 'birch'. [***beeth***]

Belhelvie (Aberdeenshire) *Balhelvy* 1538 perhaps 'Selbach's farm' from Gaelic *baile* 'farm, settlement' and the Gaelic personal name *Sealbhach*, meaning 'rich in possessions'. [*bel-**hel**-vee*]

Bellabeg (Aberdeenshire) *Bellabeg* 1494 'little farm' from Gaelic *baile* 'farm, settlement' and *beag* 'small'. [***bel**-a-**beg***]

Belnacraig (Aberdeenshire) *Balnacraig* 1545 'farm by the rock' from Gaelic *baile* 'farm, settlement' *na* 'by the' *creige* (from *creag*) 'rock, crag'. [*bel-na-**craig***]

Bernera, Berneray (Highland, Western Isles) *Berneray* 1654 (H), *Bernera* 1654 (WI) 'Bjorn's island' or 'bear island' from the Old Norse personal name *Björn* or the related word *björn* 'bear' and *ey* 'island'. [***ber**-ner-a*]

Bettyhill (Highland) named after Elizabeth Leveson-Gower, a nineteenth-century Countess (later Duchess) of Sutherland, who is perhaps best known for her involvement in the Highland Clearances. [*bet-ee-**hill***]

Birgham (Borders) *Brygham* 1095 'bridge village' from Old English *brycg* 'bridge' and *hām* 'homestead, village'. [***bir**-jam*]

Bishopbriggs (East Dunbartonshire) *Bischoprigis* 1702 'the bishop's riggs' from Scots *bishop* and *rigg* 'ridge, strip of cultivated land'. The modern spelling indicates that the second element was mistaken for Scots *brig* 'bridge'. [*bish-op-**riggz***]

Blair Atholl (Perth & Kinross) *Athfhotla* 739 'plain in Atholl' from Gaelic *blàr* 'field, plain' and the district name *Atholl*, which means 'new Ireland' from Gaelic *ath* 'new, second' and *Fótla*, a poetic name for Ireland. [*blair-**ath**-ol*]

Blairgowrie (Perth & Kinross) *Blair in Gowrie* 1656 'plain in Gowrie' from Gaelic *blàr* 'field, plain' and the district name *Gowrie*, derived from the name of the sixth-century Gaelic king *Gabrán*. [*blair-**gow**-ree*]

Blinkbonny (Fife, Midlothian) This Scots name literally means a place with a good or *bonny* view. [*blink-**bonn**-ee*]

Bonar Bridge (Highland) *Bunnach* 1275, *Bonar* 1674 'bridge over the bottom ford' from Gaelic *bonn* 'foot, bottom, foundation' and *àth* 'ford', to which Scots *bridge* was added with the completion of Thomas Telford's bridge in 1812. [*boan-ar-**bridge***]

Bonawe (Argyll & Bute) *Bunawe* 1750 'mouth of the river Awe' from Gaelic *bun* 'foot, bottom' and the river name *Awe* derived from *abh* 'stream, river'. [*bon-**awe***]

Bo'ness (West Lothian) *(The) Nes* 1494, *Burustounness* 1532 'headland of Borrowstoun'. Bo'ness was originally known simply as Ness, from Old English *næss* 'head-land', but then became Borrowstounness in reference to the adjacent village of Borrowstoun, whose meaning is perhaps 'Beornweard's farm' from the Old English personal name *Beornweard* and *tūn* 'village, farm, estate'. The name was eventually shortened to Bo'ness. [*boa-**ness***]

Bonhill (West Dunbartonshire) *Buthelulle* 1247–59 'church of Lolanus' from Gaelic *both* 'hut, church' and the name of the obscure saint *Lolanus*. [*bon-**hill***]

Bonnington (East Lothian, Midlothian) *Bondingtoun(e)* 1329–71 (EL), *Bondingtona* c.1315 (ML) 'peasant farm' from the plural form of Old Norse *bóndi* or Old English *bonda* 'peasant, serf, bondman' and Old English *tūn* 'village, farm, estate'. [***bon**-ing-tun*]

Bonnyrigg (Midlothian) *Bannockrig* 1773 'bannock-shaped ridge' from Scots *bannock* 'a round flat cake' and *rigg* 'ridge, narrow hill'. [***bon**-ee-rig*]

Borgue (Dumfries & Galloway) *Worgis* c.1161–70, *Borg* 1235–53 'stronghold' from Old Norse *borg* 'stronghold, fortification'. [***borg***]

Borthwick (Borders, Midlothian) *Bordewich* 1165–69 (B), *Borthwyk* 1361 (ML) 'home farm' from Old English *bord* 'board, table' and *wīc* 'farm, settlement'. A board farm was one whose produce supplied the table or 'board' of the local lord. [***borth**-wick*]

Borve (Western Isles) *Borg* 1654 'stronghold' from Old Norse *borg* 'stronghold, fortification'. [***borv***]

Bowmore (Argyll & Bute) *Bowmore* 1820 'big reef' from Gaelic *bogha* 'submerged rock, breaker' and *mòr* 'big'. [*boa-**moar***]

Brabster (Highland) *Brabustyrmyr* 1519, **Brabuster** (Orkney) *Brabustir* 1500 'broad farm' from Old Norse *breiðr* 'broad' and *bólstaðr* 'dwelling, farmstead'. [***brab**-ster*]

Braemar (Aberdeenshire) *Bray of Marre* 1560 'the upper part of Marr' from Gaelic *bràigh* 'upland, upper part' and the district name of Marr. [*bray-**marr***]

Breadalbane (Perth & Kinross, Stirling) *Bredalban* c.1600 'the upper part of Scotland' from Gaelic *bràghad* 'upland, upper part' and *Albainn* (from *Alba*) 'Scotland'. [*bred-**al**-bin*]

Brechin (Angus) *Brechin* a.1150 '(place of) Brychan' from the Celtic personal name *Brychan.* [***breech**-in*]

Brettabister (Shetland) *Bratabuster* c.1507–13 'steep farm' from Old Norse *brattr* 'steep' and *bólstaðr* 'dwelling, farmstead'. [***brett**-a-bist-er*]

Bridge of Allan (Stirling) 'bridge over the river Allan' from Scots *bridge* which was added to an existing river-name from pre-Celtic **Alauna* 'flowing one'. [*bridge-ov-**all**-an*]

Broadford (Highland) *Broadford* 1750 'broad sea-loch' from Old Norse *breiðr* 'broad' and *fjǫrðr* 'fjord, sea-loch'. [***brod**-ford*]

Brodick (North Ayrshire) *Bradwok* 1371, *Brethwic* 1391 'broad bay' from Old Norse *breiðr* 'broad' and *vík* 'bay'. [***brod**-ick*]

Brora (Highland) *Bruray* 1601 'bridge river' from Old Norse *brú* 'bridge' (in the possessive form *brúar*) and *á* 'river'. [***broh**-ra*]

Broxburn (West Lothian) *Broxburne* 1638 'stream of the badgers' from Scots *brok, brock* 'badger' and *burn* 'stream'. [***brox**-burn*]

Buckhaven (Fife) *Bukhawyne* 1527 perhaps 'harbour of gushing water' from Scots *buck* or *bock* 'gush, flow, retch' and *havin* 'harbour, haven'. [*buck-**haven**,* locally *buck-**hine***]

Buckie (Moray) *Buky* 1362 'gushing burn' or 'burn of the mill-sluice' from Scots *buck* or *bock* 'gush, flow, retch' or *bucky* 'the sluice of a mill-pond'. The burn in question is the Buckie Burn. [***buck**-ee*]

Burghead (Moray) *Brugh Head* 1755 'headland of the fort' possibly from Old Norse *borg* 'stronghold, fortification' or Scots *broch* 'fort' and Scots *head.* [*burg-**hedd***]

Busbie (East Ayrshire) *Busby* 1467–68, **Busby** (Renfrewshire) *Busbie* c.1300 'shrub settlement' from Old Norse *buski* 'shrubbery' and *bœr, býr* 'farm, settlement'. [*buzz-bee*]

Bute (Argyll & Bute) *Bot* 1093, *Boot* 1292 perhaps '(island of) fire' from old Gaelic *bód* 'fire', possibly in reference to signal fires. [*byoot*]

Cadboll (Highland) *Kattepol* 1281 'wildcat farm' from Old Norse *köttr* 'cat' and *ból* 'farm'. [*cad-bul*]

Caithness (Highland) *Kathenessia* c.970 probably 'headland of the Cats' from a tribal name for the local Celtic people and Old Norse *nes* 'headland'. [*caith-ness*]

Callander (Stirling) *Kalentar* c.1150, *Calentare* 1450 '(place by) the hard water' from Brittonic/Pictish **caleto-* 'hard' and **dubro* 'water'. [*cal-an-dur*]

Callanish (Western Isles) *Classerniss* 1695, *Callarnish* 1750 'the caller's promontory' from Old Norse *kallaðr* 'a caller' and *nes* 'headland'. The name refers to a headland where travellers called for a ferryboat across the water. [*cal-a-nish*]

Cambuslang (South Lanarkshire) *Camboslanc* 1296, *Cambuslange* 1379–81 'the river bend of the ships' from Gaelic *camas* 'bay, mooring, river bend' and *long* 'ship'. [*cam-bus-lang*]

Campbeltown (Argyll & Bute) 'Campbell's town', named after Archibald Campbell, the Earl of Argyle, who was granted the right to form a burgh here in 1667. [*cam-bil-town*]

Canisbay (Highland) *Cananesbi* 1225–45 'Canan's settlement' from the genitive form of an obscure, possibly Pictish personal name *Cano* and Old Norse *bœr, býr* 'farm, settlement'. The *Clan Channan* are recorded in early records as local landowners. [*can-iss-bee*]

Cannich (Highland) *Inverchaynayas* 1513, *Inverchanais* 1538–39 This has been interpreted as '(place of) bog cotton' from Gaelic *canach* 'cotton grass, bog cotton', but the historical forms reveal that this was originally a river name, making this explanation somewhat unlikely. [*can-ich*]

Canonbie (Dumfries & Galloway) *Cannaby* 1275, *Canonby* 1296 'Canons' settlement' from Middle English *cano(u)n* and Old Norse *bœr, býr* 'farm, settlement'. A priory was founded here in the twelfth century. [*can-on-bee*]

Cape Wrath (Highland) *Wraith* 1583 'headland of the turning point' from Old Norse *hvarf* 'turning point' to which English *cape* 'headland' was later added. [*cape-rath*]

Carloway (Western Isles) *Kadlowa* 1583, *Carlowa* 1750 'Karl's bay' from the Old Norse personal name *Karl* and *vágr* 'bay'. [*carl-uh-way*]

Carrick (South Ayrshire) *Karric* 1153 'rock' from Brittonic *carreg*, borrowed into Gaelic as *carraig*. [*car-ick*]

Carstairs (South Lanarkshire) *Casteltarras* 1172 'castle of Tarres' perhaps from Gaelic *caisteal* or Older Scots *castel* and the personal name *Tarres*. [*car-stairs*]

Ceres (Fife) *Sires* 1140–52 'western place' from Gaelic *siar* 'west, westerly' with an *–es* locational ending meaning 'place of'. [*see-res*]

Clackmannan (Clackmannanshire) *Clacmanan* 1147 'stone of Manau' from Brittonic *clog* 'stone' and the district name *Manau* meaning 'projecting or high land'. [*clack-man-an*]

Claggan (Highland) *Claggan* 1820 'the skull' from Gaelic *claigeann* 'skull, skull-shaped hill'. [*clagg-an*]

Clashindarroch (Aberdeenshire) 'the ditch by the oak trees' from Gaelic *clais* 'ditch, hollow' *an* 'by the' and *dairach* (from *darach*) 'oak'. [*clash-in-dar-och*]

Clashmore (Highland) *Clashmore* 1661 'the big ditch' from Gaelic *clais* 'ditch, hollow' and *mòr* 'big'. [*clash-moar*]

Clashnessie (Highland) *Clash Nessan* 1755 'the ditch by the waterfall' from Gaelic *clais* 'ditch, hollow' *an* 'by the' and *easa* (from *eas*) 'waterfall, rapids'.[*clash-**ness**-ee*]

Clydebank (West Dunbartonshire) 'bank of the River Clyde' from Scots *bank* and the river name *Clyde*, which is believed to contain the name of the Celtic river goddess *Clota*. This modern name evolved in the nineteenth century, when the Thomson brothers moved their 'Clyde Bank' foundry and shipbuilding yard from Finnieston in Glasgow to larger premises along the Dunbartonshire shore. [*clide-**bank***]

Coatbridge (North Lanarkshire) *Cottis* 1545, *Cottbrig* 1755 'Colts' bridge' from the Anglo-Norman surname *Colet* and Scots *bridge*. The Colt family (often pronounced as 'Coat' locally) were landowners in the area from the thirteenth century onwards. [*coat-**bridge***]

Coatdyke (North Lanarkshire) *Cowdyke* 1755 'Colts' wall' from the Anglo-Norman surname *Colet* and Scots *dyke* 'wall'. The 'dyke' here refers to the eastern boundary of the Colt family's estate. [*coat-**dike***]

Coldingham (Borders) *Coldingaham* c.1125 either 'village of Colud's followers' or 'village of the settlers near Colud' from either a personal name or a place-name *Colud*, as also found in the nearby place-name *Coludesburh* (recorded c.679, but now lost), together with Old English *inga* 'of the settlers' and *hām* 'homestead, village'. [***coal**-ding-am*]

Coldstream (Borders) *Caldestream* c.1210 'cold stream' from Old English *cald, ceald* 'cold' and *strēam* 'stream, brook'. The stream in question may be the Leet Water. [***cold**-stream*]

Colintraive (Argyll & Bute) *Coulintry* 1755 perhaps 'the strait of the swimming' from Gaelic *caol(as)* 'strait, sound' *an t-* 'of the' *snàimh* (from *snàmh*) 'swimming'. Cattle were swum across the narrows here. [*col-in-**trive***]

Coupar Angus (Perth & Kinross) *Cubre* 1306–29, *Cowper* 1653 'confluence (of Angus)' from Pictish **cupar* 'confluence', to which the district name *Angus* was subsequently added to distinguish it from Cupar in Fife. [***coo**-pir*]

Cowal (Argyll & Bute) *Cowalle* 1375–76 'Comgall's (land)' from the name of the sixth-century ruler of Dál Riata, *Comgall mac Domangairt*, a grandson of the legendary Fergus Mór. [***cow**-al*]

Cowdenbeath (Fife) *Codane Beitht* 1507 'Cowden's part of Beath'. The Cowden family held lands in Beath, a Gaelic place-name from *beithe* 'birch'. [*cow-din-**beeth***]

Coylumbridge (Highland) 'bridge at the gorge-leap' from Gaelic *cuingleum* 'gorge-leap', to which Scots *bridge* was later added. [*coy-lum-**bridge***]

Crail (Fife) *Crale* 1314-18 'rocky stronghold' from Pictish *caer* 'fort, stronghold' and a Pictish element derived from the Celtic root *al-* 'rock'. [***crail***]

Crailing (Borders) *Craling* 1147–50 'the nook of the slope' from Old English **crā*, cognate with Old Norse *krá* 'nook, corner' and Old English *hlinc* 'slope, ridge'. [***cray**-ling*]

Creetown (Dumfries & Galloway) *Crethe* 1301 'town on the river Cree' from the river name *Cree* from Gaelic *crìoch* 'boundary' and Scots *town.* [***cree**-tun*]

Crianlarich (Stirling) *Creinlarach* 1603 'the withered site' from Gaelic *crìon* 'withered, little' and *làrach* 'site of a house, ruin'. [*cree-in-**lar**-ich*]

Crieff (Perth & Kinross) *Creffe* a.1178 'place of trees' from Gaelic *craobh* 'tree'. [***creef***]

Cromarty (Highland) *Crumbathyn* 1263, *Crumbauchtyn* 1264, *Crumbhartyn* 1296 This name is obscure. The first element is likely to be Gaelic *crom* 'crooked' and one possible interpretation of the second part of the name is Gaelic *bath* 'sea' and the locative ending *–in* 'place of', giving the meaning 'crooked (place by) the sea', although this is highly speculative. [***crom**-ur-tee*]

Crosbie (North Ayrshire) *Crosby* a.1214 'cross farm' from Old Norse *kross* 'cross' and *bœr, býr* 'farm, settlement'. [***croz**-bee*]

Croy (Highland, North Lanarkshire, South Ayrshire) *Croy* 1473 (H), *Croy* 1373–74 (NL), *Croy* 1369 (SA) 'hard place' from Gaelic *cruaidh* 'hard, firm'. [***croy***]

Cullen (Moray) *Inverculan* c.1190, *Culane* 1381–82 'mouth of the river Cullen' from Gaelic *inbhir* 'river mouth, confluence' and the river-name *Cullen,* meaning 'holly (stream)' from Gaelic *cuileann* 'holly'. Cullen was originally known as Invercullen. [***cull**-in*]

Culloden (Highland) *Cullodyn* 1556–61 'nook of the pool or marsh' from Gaelic *cùil* 'nook, corner' and *lodair* 'pool, marsh'. The Battle of Culloden, fought here in 1746, was the last battle fought on British soil. [*cull-**odd**-in*]

Culross (Fife) *Culenros* c.1200 'holly promontory' from Gaelic *cuileann* 'holly' and *ros* 'point, promontory'. [***coo**-ross*]

Cumbernauld (North Lanarkshire) *Cumbirnald* 1373–74 'meeting of the burns' from Gaelic *comar* 'meeting, confluence' *na* 'of the' *allt* 'burn, stream'. [*cum-ber-**nawld***]

Cupar (Fife) *Cupre* 1183 'confluence' from Pictish **cupar* 'confluence'. [***coo**-pir*]

Currie (Edinburgh) *Curri* 1336 'marshy place' from the dative form of Gaelic *currach* 'marsh'. [***curr**-ay*]

Dalbeattie (Dumfries & Galloway) *Dalbaty* 1469 possibly 'meadow of the birchwood' from Gaelic *dail* 'field, meadow' and *beitheach* 'birchwood', or more probably 'drowned meadow' with the second element being *bhàite* (from *bàite*) 'drowned', in the sense of 'liable to flooding'. [*dal-**beet**-ee*]

Dalgety Bay (Fife) *Dalgathin* 1179 'bay of Dalgety' from the Gaelic name *Dalgety*, meaning 'place of thorns' from *dealg* 'thorn' *atu/etu* and *–in*, combining to mean 'place of', to which Scots *bay* was subsequently added. [*dal-ge-tee-**bay***]

Dalkeith (Midlothian) *Dolchet* 1144 'wooded meadow' from Brittonic *dol, dul* 'field, meadow, dale' and **cēt* 'wood'. [*dal-**keeth**,* locally *daw-**keeth***]

Dallas (Moray) *Dolays* 1232 'meadow station' from Pictish *dol, dul* 'field, meadow, dale' and *gwas* 'abode, dwelling' related to Gaelic *fas* 'station, place, level spot'. Alternatively, the second element may be a locational suffix meaning 'place at', giving an overall meaning of '(place at) the meadow'. [***dall**-us*]

Dalnaspidal (Perth & Kinross) *Dalnaspidel* 1750 'meadow of the hospice' from Gaelic *dail* 'field, meadow' *na* 'of the' *spideil* (from *spideal*) '(mountain) hospice for travellers'. [*dal-na-**spitt**-al*]

Dalry (Dumfries & Galloway, Midlothian, North Ayshire) *Dalri* c.1275 (DG), *Dalry* c.1328 (ML), *Dalry* 1315 (NA) perhaps 'heather meadow' from Gaelic *dail* 'field, meadow' and *fhraoich* (from *fraoch*) 'heather'. [*dal-**rye***]

Dalserf (South Lanarkshire) *Dalserff* 1406–07 'St Serf's meadow' from Gaelic *dail* 'field, meadow' and the name of the Celtic saint *Serf (Servanus)*. [*dal-**serf***]

Dalswinton (Dumfries & Galloway) *Dalswynton* 1290 '(water-) meadow of Swinton' from the existing place-name *Swinton* 'pig-farm' containing Old English *swīn* 'swine, pig' and *tūn* 'village, farm, estate', to which Gaelic *dail* 'field, meadow' in this sense a haugh or water-meadow, was subsequently added. [*dal-**swin**-tun*]

Dalton (Dumfries & Galloway) *Delton* c.1280 'farm in the valley' from Old English *dæl* 'valley' and *tūn* 'village, farm, estate'. [***dol**-tun*]

Dalwhinnie (Highland) *Dalwhiny* 1750 perhaps 'meadow of the champions' from Gaelic *dail* 'field, meadow' and a Gaelic word related to Early Irish *cuinnid* 'champion'. [*dal-**whin**-ee*]

Darnick (Borders) *Dernewic* c.1136 'hidden farm' from Old English *derne* 'secret, hidden' and *wīc* 'farm, settlement'. [***darn**-ick*]

Dingwall (Highland) *Dingwell* 1227 'assembly field' from Old Norse *þing* 'assembly place, parliament' and *vǫllr* 'field, level ground'. [***ding**-wall*]

Dollar (Clackmannanshire) *Dolair* 10thC 'place of the water-meadow' from Brittonic *dol, dul* 'field, (water) meadow, dale' and an *-ar* suffix meaning 'place of'. [***doll**-ar*]

Dores (Highland) *Durris*, 1263, *Durrys* 1530 'black woods' from Gaelic *dubh* 'black' and *ros* 'woodland, point'. [***doarz***]

Dornoch (Highland) *Durnach* 1140–45 'pebbly place' from Gaelic *dòrnach* 'place of pebbles', derived from *dòrn* 'fist, fist-sized pebble'. [***dorn**-ach*]

Dounreay (Highland) *Ra* 1225, *Dounrae* 1654 'fort at the corner or elevation' from Gaelic *dùn* 'fortified place' which was added to the existing place-name *Reay*, formed from Old Norse *(v)rá* 'corner' or *rá* 'a pole' used here in the sense of 'a long stretched-out elevation'. [*doon-**ray***, locally ***doon**-ray*]

Drumbuie (Highland) *Drumboy* 1509 'yellow ridge' from Gaelic *druim* 'ridge' and *buidhe* 'yellow'. [*drum-**boo**-ee*]

Drumnadrochit (Highland) *Drumindrochit* 1820 'ridge of the bridge' from Gaelic *druim* 'ridge' *na* 'of the' and *drochaide* (from *drochaid*) 'bridge'. [*drum-na-**droch**-it*]

Drumochter (Highland) *Druinochtyr* 1732 'summit of the ridge' from Gaelic *druim* 'ridge' and *uachdair* (from *uachdar*) 'summit, upper part'. [*drum-**och**-tir*]

Dryburgh (Borders) *Driburgh* c.1150 'dry fort' from Old English *drȳge* 'dry' and *burh* 'fortified place'. [*dry-burr-a*]

Drymen (Stirling) *Drumyn* 1238 'ridge place' from Gaelic *druim* 'ridge'. [***drim**-in*]

Dufftown (Moray) 'Duff's town' This name commemorates James Duff, 4th Earl of Fife, who founded the town in 1817. The older name was Balvenie. [***duff**-tun*]

Dullatur (North Lanarkshire) *Dullatt(ur)* 1553 'the dark hillside' from Gaelic *dubh* 'dark, black' and *leitir* 'steep slope, hillside'. [***dull**-a-turr*]

Dumbarton (West Dunbartonshire) *Dunbretane* a.1445 'fort of the Briton(s)' from Gaelic *dùn* 'fortified place' and *Breatan* 'Briton'. Dumbarton Rock was the stronghold of the Brittonic-speaking Britons. [*dum-**bar**-tin*]

Dumfries (Dumfries & Galloway) *Dunfres* 1189 'fort of the copse(s)' from Gaelic *dùn* 'fortified place' and *phris* (from *preas*) 'copse, thicket'. [*dum-**freece***]

Dunbar (East Lothian) *Dynbaer* c.709 'summit fort' from Gaelic *dùn* 'fortified place' and *bàrr* 'top, summit'. The Gaelic form is likely to have replaced an earlier Brittonic form *din-bar* with the same meaning. [*dun-**bar***]

Dunblane (Stirling) *Dul Blaan* 9thC, *Dumblann* c.1200 'fort of St Blane' from Gaelic *dùn* 'fortified place' and the name of the Gaelic saint *Bláán*, although the first historical form reveals that the name may originally have been 'meadow of St Blane' from Gaelic *dail* 'field, meadow, dale', or the related Brittonic word. [*dun-**blain***]

Duncansby Head (Highland) *Dungalsbaer* c.1225 'headland at Dungal's farm' from the Celtic personal name *Dungal* and Old Norse *bœr, býr* 'farm, settlement', to which Scots *head* was later added. [*dun-canz-bee-**hedd***]

Dundee (Angus) *Dunde* c.1180 'fort of Daig(h)' from Gaelic *dùn* 'fortified place' and perhaps the Old Irish personal name *Daig(h)*, which meant 'fire'. [*dun-**dee***]

Dundrennan (Dumfries & Galloway) *Dundrainan* c.1160 'hill of thorns' from Gaelic *dùn* 'fortified place, hill' and *droighnean* 'thorns'. [*dun-**drenn**-an*]

Dunfermline (Fife) *Dunfermelin* 1128 'fort of the people of Western Fife' from Gaelic *dùn* 'fortified place' and perhaps a territorial name **ferm(e)lin*, referring to the kin-group who ruled this part of *Fothrif* (West Fife) This name might contain the plural of Gaelic *fear* 'man', although a Pictish origin cannot be ruled out. [*dun-**ferm**-lin*]

Dunkeld (Perth & Kinross) *Dúin Chaillden* 873 'fort of the Caledonians' from Gaelic *dùn* 'fortified place' and *Chailleann* 'Caledonians'. [*dun-**keld***]

Dunnichen (Angus) *Dunnachtyn* a.1220 'Nechtan's fort' from Gaelic *dùn* 'fortified place' and the Celtic personal name *Nechtán (Neachdán)*. [***dun**-ee-chin*]

Dunoon (Argyll & Bute) *Dunnon* c.1240, *Dunhoven* 1270 'fort on the river' from Gaelic *dùn* 'fortified place' and *obhainn* 'river'. [*duh-**noon***]

Dunragit (Dumfries & Galloway) *Dunrechet* 9thC 'fort of Rheged' from Gaelic *dùn* 'fortified place' and the name of the British kingdom of *Rheged*, which extended across much of South-West Scotland. [*dun-**rag**-it*]

Duntocher (West Dunbartonshire) *Drumthocher* 1225–70, *Drumtochir* 1580–81 'fort at the causeway' from Gaelic *dùn* 'fortified place' and *tochar* 'causeway, road'. The historical forms reveal that the first element was originally Gaelic *druim* 'ridge'. [*dun-**toch**-er*]

Durness (Highland) *Dyrnes* c.1230 'deer headland' from Old Norse *dýr* 'deer' and *nes* 'headland'. [*dur-**ness***]

Dysart (Fife) *Disart* 1220 'the hermitage' from Gaelic *diseart* 'hermitage, religious retreat'. [***die**-sart*]

Earlsferry (Fife) *Erlsferie* c.1296 This name refers to the historical ferry which linked eastern Fife with North Berwick, instituted by the Earls of Fife for the use of pilgrims travelling to the shrine of St Andrew. [***erls**-ferr-ay*]

Earlston (Borders) *Ercheldon* c.1143–44 'Earcil's hill' from an Old English personal name *Earcil* and *dūn* 'hill'. Alternatively, the first element may have been an existing Brittonic place-name. [***erl**-stun*]

East Kilbride (South Lanarkshire) *Killebride* 1181 '(eastern) church of St Brigid' from Gaelic *cill* 'church' and one of the sixteen Celtic saints named *Brigid*. 'East' was added later to distinguish the town from West Kilbride in North Ayrshire. [*east-kil-**bride***]

East Linton (East Lothian) *Lintun* 1127 '(eastern) flax farm' from Old English *līn* 'flax' and *tūn* 'village, farm, estate'. 'East' was added later to distinguish the town from West Linton in the Borders. [*east-**lin**-tun*]

Ecclefechan (Dumfries & Galloway) *Eggleffychan* 1296 either 'church of St Fechin' from Gaelic *eaglais* 'church' and the name of the Celtic saint *Fechin*, or 'small church' from Brittonic *eglēs* 'church' and *bechan* (mutated to *fechan*) 'small'. [*ek-ell-**fech**-an*]

Ecclesmachan (West Lothian) *Egglesmanekin* 1207, *Eglismauchin* 1540 'church of St Machan' from Brittonic *eglēs* or Gaelic *eaglais* 'church' and the name of the Celtic saint *Machan*. [*ek-ells-**mach**-an*]

Edinburgh (Edinburgh) *Eidyn* c.600, *Edenburge* 1126 'fort of Eidyn' The old Brittonic name was *Din Eidyn* from *din* 'fort, fortification' and the obscure name *Eidyn*. *Din* was later replaced by Old English *burh*, which has the same meaning. [***ed**-in-burr-a*]

Ednam (Borders) *Ædnaham* c.1105 'village on the Eden' from the river-name *Eden* and Old English *hām* 'homestead, village'. [***ed**-nam*]

Edrom (Borders) *Edrem, Ederham* 1095 'village on the Adder' from the river-name *Adder* (now known as *Whiteadder*) and Old English *hām* 'homestead, village'. [***ed**-rom*]

Eigg (Highland) *Egge* 1292 'notched isle' from Gaelic *eag* 'notch, gap'. [***egg***]

Eilean Donan (Highland) *Elandonan* c.1425 'St Donnan's Isle' from Gaelic *eilean* 'island' and the name of the Gaelic saint *Donnán* who was martyred on the isle of Eigg in 617 AD. [*ay-lan-**don**-an*]

Elgin (Moray) *Elgin* 1136 'little Ireland' from *Elg*, an old name for Ireland with the diminutive suffix *–in* 'little'. The name seems to reflect the settlement of Gaelic speakers from Ireland in what had previously been Pictish territory. [***elg**-in*]

Ellon (Aberdeenshire) *Helain* 1131–32, *Ellon* 1157 'meadow' from Gaelic *eilean* 'island, (water) meadow'. [***ell**-an*]

Elrick (Aberdeenshire) *Elrik* 1529, **Elrig** (Dumfries & Galloway) *Elrig* 1657 'deer trap' from Gaelic *eileirg* 'deer trap'. [***ell**-rick, **ell**-rig*]

Embo (Highland) *Ethenboll* c.1230, *Eyndboll* 1610 The first element is unclear but it probably an Old Norse personal name. The second element is Old Norse *ból* 'farm'. [***em**-bo*]

Eskadale (Highland) *Aeskedaell* 1568 'ash-tree valley' from Old Norse *eski*, developed from *askr* 'ash-woodland' and *dalr* 'valley'. [***esk**-a-dail*]

Evanton (Highland) 'Evan's town'. The name commemorates local nineteenth-century landowner Evan Fraser of Balconie. [***ev**-an-tun*]

Evelix (Highland) *Aveleche* 1222 'the ember' from Gaelic *éibhleag* 'ember' with an English *–s* plural. The name refers to the sparkling Evelix burn. [***ee**-va-licks*]

Eyemouth (Borders) *Aymuth* c.1300 'mouth of the river Eye'. The river name derives from Old English *ēa* 'river' to which *mūða* 'mouth' was added. [***eye**-mouth*]

Fair Isle (Shetland) *Fároy* 1350 'sheep island' from Old Norse *fár* 'sheep' and *ey* 'island', later replaced by Scots *isle.* [***fair**-ile*]

Falkirk (Falkirk) *Egglesbreth* c.1120, *Faukirk* 1298 'speckled church' from Scots *faw* 'speckled, multi-coloured' and *kirk* 'church'. This is a translation of the older Gaelic name *Egglesbreth*, from *eaglais* 'church' and *breac* 'speckled'. [***fol**-kirk*, locally ***faw**-kirk*]

Fasnacloich (Argyll & Bute) *Fasnacloich* 1750 'stance of the stone' from Gaelic *fas* 'station, place, level spot' *na* 'of the' *cloiche* (from *clach*) 'stone'. [*fass-na-**cloych***]

Fasnakyle (Highland) *Fasnakyle* 1807 'stance by the wood' from Gaelic *fas* 'station, place, level spot' *na* 'of the' *coille* 'wood'. [*fass-na-**kyle***]

Fauldhouse (West Lothian) *Fawlhous* 1523, *Faldhous* 1559–60 'house on fallow land' from Old English *fealh, falh* 'fallow land' and *hūs* 'house', although subsequent historical forms show influence from Scots *fauld* 'fold, animal enclosure'. [***fauld**-house*]

Fearn (Highland) *Ferne* 1529 'place of alders' from Gaelic *feàrna* 'alder tree'. [***fern***]

Fenwick (Borders) *ffenwic* c.1280 'bog farm' from Old English *fenn* 'bog, marsh, fen' and *wīc* 'farm, settlement'. [**fen**-ick]

Fetterangus (Aberdeenshire) *Fethiranus* 1207 'Angus's slope' or 'Angus's district' from Gaelic *fothair* which may mean 'terraced slope' or may instead be a loan-word from Pictish **uotir* 'district, region' and the Gaelic personal name *Aonghais.* [*fett-er-**ang**-gus*]

Fettercairn (Aberdeenshire) *Fothercardine, Fettercardin* 1324–71 'slope of the thicket' or 'district of the thicket' from Gaelic *fothair* which may mean 'terraced slope' or may instead be a loanword from Pictish **uotir* 'district, region', and Pictish *carrden* 'thicket'. [*fett-er-**cairn***]

Fetteresso (Aberdeenshire) *Fodresach* 10thC, *Fethiresach* c.1251 'waterfall slope' or 'waterfall district' from Gaelic *fothair* which may mean 'terraced slope' or may instead be a loanword from Pictish **uotir* 'district, region' and the adjective *easach* from *eas* 'waterfall, rapids'. [*fett-er-**ess**-o*]

Findhorn (Moray) *Fyndorn* 1595 '(place on) the river Findhorn' from the river-name *Findhorn* containing Gaelic *fionn* 'white' and either *Éireann* 'Ireland' or a pre-Celtic root **Ara-* meaning 'water-course'. [***finnd**-horn*]

Finnart (Argyll & Bute, Perth & Kinross) *Fynnard* a.1350 (AB), *Fingart* 1820 (PK) 'white promontory' from Gaelic *fionn* 'white' and *àird, àrd* 'height, promontory'. [***fin**-art*]

Fintry (Aberdeenshire, Stirling) *Fintrefe* c.1219 (A), *Fyntrif* a.1225 (S) 'white farm' from Gaelic *fionn* 'white' and Brittonic/Pictish *tref* 'farm, settlement'. *Fionn* may well replace earlier Brittonic/Pictish cognate *gwen* with the same meaning. [***fint**-ree*]

Fionnphort (Argyll & Bute) 'white harbour' from Gaelic *fionn* 'white' and *phort* (from *port*) 'harbour, ferry'. [***finn**-a-fort*]

Firth of Forth (East Lothian, Fife) *Forthin* c.970, *Foirthe* 1120, *Myrkvafirði* c.1200 'estaury of the river Forth' from the river-name *Forth*, derived from Celtic **uo-rit-ia* 'slow-running (one)'. The firth was also known as *Myrkvafjǫrðr* in Old Norse, containing *myrkva* (from *myrkvi*) 'mirky, foggy' and and *firði* (from *fjǫrðr*) 'fjord, sea-loch', and the 'Firth' part of the name may be a remnant from this period, although *fjǫrðr* was borrowed into Scots as *firth* and as such may be a later addition. [*firth-ov-**forth***]

Fochabers (Moray) *Fochoper* 1124, *Fochabris* 1514 This name is obscure. The second element may be Pictish *aber* 'river mouth, confluence', but the intial element is unclear. [***foch**-a-burz*]

Forfar (Angus) *Forfare* 1492–93 possibly 'ridge of the terraces' from Gaelic *fothair* 'terraced slope' and *fàire* 'ridge', although this is uncertain. [***for**-far*]

Forres (Moray) *Forais* 1189–99 'the underwood' from Gaelic *fo* 'under, below' and *ras* 'shrubbery, underwood'. [***for**-iss*]

Fort Augustus (Highland) This eighteenth-century fort was named in honour of William Augustus, Duke of Cumberland. The Gaelic name is *Cill Chuimein* 'St Cumméin's church'. [*for-ta-**gust**-us*]

Fort George (Highland) This eighteenth-century fort was named in honour of King George II. [*fort-**jorge***]

Fortrose (Highland) *Forterose* 1445 'below the headland' from Gaelic *foter* 'under, beneath' and *ros* 'point, promontory'. [*for-**troase***]

Fort William (Highland) This seventeenth-century fort was named in honour of King William III. The Gaelic name is *An Gearasdan* 'the garrsion', or *Gearasdan Inbhir-lochaidh* 'the Inverlochy Garrison'. [*fort-**will**-yam*]

Foula (Shetland) *Fule* 1654 'bird island' from Old Norse *fugl* 'bird, fowl' and *ey* 'island'. [***fool**-ah*]

Foulis, Fowlis (Angus, Highland, Perth & Kinross) *Fowlis* 1517 (A), *Foulis* 1381 (H), *Fowlis* c.1195, *Fougles* c.1198 (PK) 'lesser stream' from Gaelic *foghlais* 'sub-stream, rivulet'. [***fowlz***]

Foyers (Highland) *Foir* 1745 perhaps 'terraced slopes' from Gaelic *fothair* 'terraced slope' with an English plural added. [***foy**-erz*]

Fraserburgh (Aberdeenshire) *Faithly* 1478, *Fraserisburghe* 1595–96 'Fraser's burgh'. This name commemorates Sir Alexander Fraser, who was granted a charter raising the town to burgh status in the sixteenth century. Prior to this, Fraserburgh was known as Faithlie. Locals refer to the town as 'The Broch'. [***fray**-zer-burr-a*]

Gairloch (Highland) *Gerloth* 1275, *Garloch* 1574 'short sea-inlet' from Gaelic *geàrr* 'short' and *loch* 'lake, sea-inlet'. [*gair-loch*]

Galashiels (Borders) *Galuschel* c.1360 'shieling huts by the Gala Water' from Middle English *schele* 'shepherd's hut' and the river name *Gala*, whose meaning is unknown. [*ga-la-**sheels***]

Gare Loch (Argyll & Bute) *Gerloch* 1272 'short sea-inlet' from Gaelic *geàrr* 'short' and *loch* 'lake, sea-inlet'. [*gair-loch*]

Garmond (Aberdeenshire) *Garmond* 1820 'rough hill' from Gaelic *garbh* 'rough, coarse' and *monadh* 'mountain, hill, moor'. [***gar**-mond*]

Gartmore (Stirling) *Gartmore* 1750 'big enclosure' Gaelic *gart* '(corn)field, enclosed land' and *mòr* 'big'. [*gart-**moar***]

Gartsherrie (North Lanarkshire) *Gartsharie* 1593 'colt field' from Gaelic *gart* 'field, enclosed land' and *searraich* 'colts, foals'. [*gart-**sherr**-ee*]

Garve (Highland) 'rough place' from Gaelic *garbh* 'rough, coarse'. [***garv***]

Gatehouse of Fleet (Dumfries & Galloway) *Flete* 1300 'roadside house by the river Fleet' from Scots *gate* 'road' and *hous* 'house', and the river-name *Fleet* from Old English *flēot* or Old Norse *fljótr* 'stream, inlet'. [*gait-house-ov-**fleet***]

Girvan (South Ayrshire) *Girven* 1275 Possible interpretations of this name include 'short river' from Gaelic *geàrr* 'short' and *abhainn* 'river', or that it contains Gaelic *gar*, *garan* 'a thicket'. A further possibility is 'rough river' from the Brittonic root *garw* 'rough' and the locational ending **-ona*. [***gir**-vin*]

Glasgow (Glasgow) *Glasgu* 1136 'green hollow' from Brittonic *glas* 'green' and *cau* 'hollow'. [***glaz**-go*]

Glen Affric (Highland) *Auffrik* 1538 'valley of the river Affric' from Gaelic *gleann* 'narrow valley' and the river-name *Affric* from *ath-* 'very' and *breac* 'speckled'. [*glen-**aff**-rick*]

Glencaple (Dumfries & Galloway) *Glencaple* a.1240 'horse valley' from Gaelic *gleann* 'narrow valley' and *capall* 'horse, mare'. [*glen-**kay**-pil*]

Glencoe (Highland) *Glenagwe* c.1323, *Glenchomure* 1343, *Glencowyn* 1500 'valley of the river Coe' from Gaelic *gleann* 'narrow valley' and the obscure river-name *Coe*. The historical forms are inconsistent, but in modern Gaelic the second element has become *comhann* 'narrow'. [*glen-**co***]

Glenluce (Dumfries & Galloway) *Glenlus* 1296 'valley of the river Luce' from Gaelic *gleann* 'narrow valley' and the river-name *Luce* from *lus* 'a plant, a herb'. [*glen-**loose***]

Glenrothes (Fife) 'valley of Rothes'. This 'new town' was established in 1948 to house workers from the Rothes Colliery, which was named after local landowners the Earls of Rothes. [*glen-**roth**-us*]

Glenshee (Perth & Kinross) *Glenschee* 1495 perhaps 'fairy valley' from Gaelic *gleann* 'narrow valley' and *sìdh, sìth* 'fairy'. [*glen-**shee***]

Golspie (Highland) *Goldespy* 1330 perhaps 'Gulli's farm' from the Old Norse personal name *Gulli* and *bœr, býr* 'farm, settlement'. [***goll**-spee*]

Gorebridge (Midlothian) *Gorebridge* 1854 'bridge over the Gore' from the *Gore Water*, which may derive from Scots *gore* 'a furrow' or *gor(e)* 'slime, dirt', and Scots *bridge*. [***gore**-bridge*]

Gourock (Inverclyde) *Gowrockis* 1661 'rounded hillock' from Gaelic *guireag* 'a pimple'. [***goo**-rock*]

Grangemouth (Stirling) 'mouth of the Grange burn'. This eighteenth-century town is named from the *Grange Burn*, which in turn is named after the grange at Newbattle Abbey, from Scots *grange* 'granary, barn'. [***grange**-muth*]

Grantown-on-Spey (Highland) 'Grant's town (on the river Spey)'. The village was planned in 1765 by local landowner James Grant. The river-name *Spey* is obscure, and may be pre-Celtic. [***gran***-*tun-on-spay*]

Greenlaw (Borders) *Grenlaw* c.1170 'green hill' from Old English *grēne* 'green' and *hlāw* 'rounded hill'. [***green***-*law*]

Greenock (Inverclyde) *Grenok* c.1395 'sunny hillock' from Gaelic *grianàg* 'sunny knoll, hillock'. [***green***-*uck*]

Gretna Green (Dumfries & Galloway) *Gretenhou* 1215–45 'green of the gravelly ridge' from Old English *grēoten* 'gravelly' and *hōh* 'heel, ridge', to which *green* was later added. [*grett-na-****green***]

Grimshader (Western Isles) *Grimsetter* 1654 'Grim's dwelling' from the Old Norse personal name *Grímr* and *setr* 'dwelling'. [***grim***-*shad-er*]

Gruinard (Highland) *Croinzneorth* 1450, *Gruinyord* 1528 'shallow firth' from Old Norse *grunn* 'shallows' and *fjǫrðr* 'fjord, sea-loch'. [***groon***-*yard*]

Gullane (East Lothian) *Golin* c.1200, *Gullen* 1659 'long ridge' from Gaelic *gualann* 'shoulder, long ridge'. [***gull***-*an*]

Habost (Western Isles) *Habost* 1662 'high farmstead' from Old Norse *hár* 'high, upper' and *bólstaðr* 'dwelling, farmstead'. [***ha***-*bost*]

Haddington (East Lothian) *Hadynton* 1098 'village of the followers of a man called Hada' from the Old English personal name *Hada* and *inga* 'of the followers' and *tūn* 'village, farm, estate'. [***had***-*ing-tun*]

Halkirk (Highland) *Hakirk* 1222 'high church' from Old Norse *hár* 'high, upper' and *kirkja* 'church'. [***hol***-*kirk*]

Hamilton (South Lanarkshire) *Hamelton* 1291 This name is from the surname *Hamilton*, the older name being *Cadzow* or *Cadihow*, whose meaning is obscure. The name may have been imported from England by Sir Walter *de Hameldone* in the thirteenth century. [***ham***-*il-tin*]

Hamnavoe (Shetland) *Hafnarvag* 12thC 'harbour bay' from Old Norse *höfn* 'haven, harbour' and *vágr* 'bay'. [*ham-na-**voe***]

Harris (Western Isles) *Heradh* c.1500, *Harrige* 1542, *Harreis* 1588 'higher (district)' or 'division'. The modern Gaelic form of this name is *Na Hearadh*, which was adapted from an Old Norse name derived from either *haerri* 'higher' or *hérað* 'county, district'. It is possible that the Scandianvian settlers in their turn adapted an existing (possibly pre-Celtic) place-name. [***harr**-iss*]

Hawick (Borders) *Hawic* 1165–69 'hedge-enclosed farm' from Old English *haga* 'hedge, enclosure' and Old English *wīc* 'farm, settlement'. [***ho**-ick*]

Helensburgh (Argyll & Bute) 'Helen's town'. This town was laid out in 1776 by Sir James Colquhoun and named in honour of his wife, Helen. [***hel**-enz-burr-a*]

Helmsdale (Highland) *Hjalmunddal* c.1225 'Hjalmund's valley' from the Old Norse personal name *Hjalmund* and *dalr* 'valley'. [***helms**-dail*]

Hobkirk (Borders) *Hoppkirck* 1654 'church in the valley' from Old English *hop* 'enclosed valley' and *cirice* 'church' (later becoming Scots *kirk*). [***hob**-kirk*]

Houston (Renfrewshire) *Villa Hugonis* c.1200, *Huston* c.1230 'Hugo's estate' from the Anglo-Norman personal name *Hugo* and Old English *tūn* 'village, farm, estate' or Scots *toun* 'farm, settlement'. The older Gaelic name was Kilpeter (from Gaelic *cill* 'church' and the name of the biblical saint *Peter*), becoming Houston when the lands were granted to Hugh of Pettinain (*Hugo de Paduinan*) in the twelfth century. [***hyoo**-stin, **hoo**-stin*]

Hoy (Orkney) *Hoye* 1492 'high island' from Old Norse *hár* 'high, upper' and *ey* 'island'. [***hoy***]

Humbie (East Lothian, Fife, Midlothian, West Lothian) *Hundeby* c.1250 (EL), *Humbies* 1517 (F), *Humby* 1546 (ML), *Hundeby* 1290 (WL) 'hound settlement' from Old Norse *hundr* 'dog, hound' and *bœr, býr* 'farm, settlement'. The name probably refers to places where hunting dogs were kept. [***hum**-bee*]

Huntly (Aberdeenshire) Huntly was named in the eighteenth century by the Earl of Huntly, whose title derives from the family's original estate of Huntly in Berwickshire, which means 'Huntsman's woodland clearing' from Old English *hunta* 'huntsman' and *lēah* 'woodland clearing'. [***hunt**-lee*]

Inchaffray (Perth & Kinross) *Incheffren* c.1190 'meadow of the offering' from Gaelic *innis* 'island, meadow' and *aifrionn* 'mass, offering'. [*insh-**aff**-ray*]

Inchcolm (Fife) *Sancti Columbe de Insula* 1162–67, *Sanct Columbis Inche* 1531 'island of St Columba' from Gaelic *innis* 'island, meadow' and the name of the Irish saint *Colm (Columba)*. This island lies in the Firth of Forth. [*insh-**coam***]

Inchinnan (Renfrewshire) *Inchenan* 1158 'meadow of St Finnan' from Gaelic *innis* 'island, meadow' and the name of the Irish saint *Finnén (Findbar)*. [*insh-**in**-an*]

Inchnadamph (Highland) *Insnadew* 1649, *Inchindaw* 1662, *Inknaduf* 1755 'meadow of the stags' from Gaelic *innis* 'island, meadow' *nan* 'of the' *daimh* (from *damh*) 'oxen, stags'. [*insh-na-**damf***]

Insh (Highland) *Inche* 1226, **Insch** (Aberdeenshire) *Inchemabanin* 1178, *Inchis* 1536 'meadow' from Gaelic *innis* 'island, meadow'. The oldest form of Insch in Aberdeenshire reveals a parochial dedication to the Celtic saint *Bean*, which is prefixed by Gaelic *mo* 'my'. [***insh***]

Inverary (Argyll & Bute) *Inverara* 1540–41, *Inverary* 1542 'mouth of the river Aray' from Gaelic *inbhir* 'river mouth, confluence' and the river-name *Aray*, which might be related to the river *Ayr*, itself a Celtic name from the root **Arā* meaning 'water-course, river'. [*in-vir-**air**-ee*]

Inverbervie (Aberdeenshire) *Haberberui* 1290 'mouth of the river Bervie' from Gaelic *inbhir* 'river mouth, confluence' and a river-name cognate with Welsh *berw* 'rushing water, boiling'. The historical form reveals that *inbhir* has replaced the cognate Pictish term *aber*. [*in-vir-**ber**-vee*]

Invergordon (Highland) *Inchbreky* 1475, *Innerbreky* 1512 Invergordon was originally known as Inverbreckie from Gaelic *inbhir* 'river mouth, confluence' and the Breckie Burn, from *breac* 'speckled'. It was renamed Invergordon in the eighteenth century by Sir William Gordon. [*in-vir-**gord**-in*]

Inverkeithing (Fife) *Hinhirkethy* 1040–57, *Inuerkethyin* 1152–59 'mouth of the Keithing' from Gaelic *inbhir* 'river mouth, confluence' and the Keithing Burn. The burn name contains Pictish **cēt* 'wood', and means 'woodland burn'. [*in-vir-**kee**-thing*]

Inverkip (Inverclyde) *Innyrkyp* c.1170 'river mouth at the stump' from Gaelic *inbhir* 'river mouth, confluence' and *ceap* 'block, stump'. [*in-vir-**kip***]

Inverness (Highland) *Invernis* a.1300 'mouth of the River Ness' from Gaelic *inbhir* 'river mouth, confluence' and an obscure Celtic or pre-Celtic river name from the root **ned-* meaning 'wet, to flood'. [*in-vir-**ness***]

Inverurie (Aberdeenshire) *Enneroury* 1172–99, *Inuerurie* 1199 'confluence of the River Urie' from Gaelic *inbhir* 'river mouth, confluence' and obscure river name *Urie*. The town stands at the confluence of the Urie and the Don. [*in-vir-**oo**-ree*]

Irvine (North Ayrshire) *Yrewyn* 1258, *Irwyn* 1296 The town takes its name from the river *Irvine*, whose meaning is obscure, although it might be related to the river *Irfon* in Wales. [***urr**-vin*]

Isbister (Orkney, Shetland) *Estirbuster* 1492 (O), *Usbuster* c.1507–13 (S) '(most) easterly farm' from Old Norse *eystri* 'easterly' and *bólstaðr* 'dwelling, farmstead'. [***iz**-bist-er*]

Jarlshof (Shetland) 'earl's temple' from Old Norse *jarl* 'earl, nobleman' and *hof* 'temple, court'. This pseudo-Norse name was created by Sir Walter Scott and used in his 1821 novel *The Pirate.* [***yarls**-hoff*]

Jedburgh (Borders) *Gedwearde* c.1050, *Jedworthe* 1147–52 'enclosure by the River Jed' from the obscure Celtic river name *Jed* and Old English *worð* 'enclosure', which was later replaced with *burgh.* [***jed**-burr-a,* locally ***jed**-art*]

Jemimaville (Highland) The village was named by Sir George Munro, fourth Laird of Poyntzfield, after his wife Jemima Charlotte Graham, whom he married in 1822. [*jeh-**my**-ma-vill*]

John o' Groats (Highland) *John o' Grott's House* 1726, *Johny Groats House* 1750 'John (o) Grott's (house)'. John Grot first mentioned in 1496 in a Caithness charter, and the Groat family appear to have been important local landowners. [*jon-o-**groats***]

Johnstone (Renfrewshire) *Jonestone* 1292 'John's farm' from the personal name *John* and Scots *toun* 'farm, settlement'. [***jon**-stun*]

Joppa (Edinburgh) This eighteenth-century name is from a local farm, which commemorates the Biblical city of Joppa. [***jopp**-a*]

Kames (Argyll & Bute, East Ayrshire) *Cameys* a.1204 (AB), *Kamis* 1541–42 (EA) The Argyll & Bute name means 'the bay' from Gaelic *camas* 'bay, mooring, river bend', whereas Kames in East Ayrshire may be 'the river bend' from the same word, or may instead be 'the ridges' from Scots *kaim, kame* 'comb, ridge'. [***kaimz***]

Keith (Moray) *Geth* 1187, *Ket* c.1220 '(place by) the wood' from Pictish **cēt* 'wood', although the name may also be associated with the local Pictish province of *Cé.* [***keeth***]

Keithick (Perth & Kinross) *Kethick* 1662, **Keithock** (Angus) *Kethik* 1492 perhaps 'small wood' from Pictish **cēt* 'wood' with the Gaelic or Pictish diminutive suffix *–oc* 'little, small'. [***keeth**-ick*]

Kelso (Borders) *Kelchehou, Calceho* 1128 'chalk ridge' from Old English *cealc* 'chalk' and *hōh* 'heel, ridge'. [***kel**-soh*]

Kerrowaird (Highland) 'the high quarter' from Gaelic *ceathramh* 'quarter' and *àrd* 'high'. [*kerr-oo-**aird***]

Kerrycroy (Argyll & Bute) *Kervycroy* 1449, *Caracroy* 1654 'the hard quarter' from Gaelic *ceathramh* 'quarter' and *cruaidh* 'hard, firm'. [*kerr-ee-**croy***]

Kershader (Western Isles) *Kersetter* 1654 'copse dwelling' from Old Norse *kjarr* 'copsewood, brushwood' and *setr* 'dwelling'. [***ker**-shad-er*]

Kilbarchan (Renfrewshire) *Kilbrauchton* 1440–41, *Kilbarchane* 1496 'church of St Berchan' from Gaelic *cill* 'church' and the name of the Celtic saint *Berchán.* [*kil-**bark**-an*]

Kilchattan (Argyll & Bute) *Killecatan* 1449 'church of St Catan' from Gaelic *cill* 'church' and the name of the Celtic saint *Catán.* [*kil-**chat**-an*]

Killiecrankie (Perth & Kinross) *Killycranky* 1750 'wood of the aspens' from Gaelic *coille* 'wood' and *critheann* 'aspen tree'. [*kil-ee-**krank**-ee*]

Killin (Stirling) *Kynlin* 1275, *Killin* 1658 possibly 'white church' from Gaelic *cill* 'church' and *fionn* 'white', although the earliest form throws doubt on this and suggests instead a name in Gaelic *ceann* 'head, end'. [*kil-**in***]

Kilmarnock (East Ayrshire) *Kelmernoke* 1299 'church of my little St Ernan' from Gaelic *cill* 'church' *mo* 'my' and the name of the Gaelic saint *Ernan* with the diminutive suffix *–oc* 'little'. [*kil-**mar**-nock*]

Kilmartin (Argyll & Bute) *Kilmarteine* 1592–93 'church of St Martin' from Gaelic *cill* 'church' and the name of the Continental saint *Martin of Tours*. [*kil-**mart**-in*]

Kilmory (Argyll & Bute, Highland) *Kilmory* 1483 (AB), *Kylmor* 1469 (H) 'Mary's church' from Gaelic *cill* 'church' and *Moir(e)*, a Gaelic form of Mary. [*kil-**moar**-ee*]

Kilmuir (Highland) *Kilmor* 1296 'Mary's church' from Gaelic *cill* 'church' and *Moir(e)*, a Gaelic form of Mary. [*kil-**myoor***]

Kilmun (Argyll & Bute) *Kylmon* 1294 'church of my dear Fintan' from Gaelic *cill* 'church' *mo* 'my' and the name of the Gaelic saint *Fintán*, in the reduced form of *Mundu* or *Munnu* (from *Mo-Findu*). [*kil-**mun***]

Kiloran (Argyll & Bute) *Killorane* 1545 'church of saint Odran' from Gaelic *cill* 'church' and the name of the Gaelic saint *Odrán*, a follower of St Columba. [*kil-**oar**-an*]

Kilsyth (North Lanarkshire) *Kelvesyth* 1210, *Kelnasydhe* 1217 This name has been interpreted as 'church of St Syth' from Gaelic *cill* 'church' and the name of a saint called *Syth*, although there are no records of such a saint. [*kil-**syth***]

Kiltarlity (Highland) *Kyltalargy*, *Kyltalargyn* 1224–26 'church of St Talorgan' from Gaelic *cill* 'church' and the name of the Pictish saint *Talorgan*. [*kil-**tar**-lit-ee*]

Kilwinning (North Ayrshire) *Killvinin* a.1160 'church of St Finnian' from Gaelic *cill* 'church' and the name of the Gaelic saint *Finnian*. [*kil-**win**-ing*]

Kincaple (Fife) *Kincapel* 1212 'the end of the horse' from Gaelic *ceann* 'head, end' and Gaelic *capall* 'horse, mare'. This may be a tribal name, referring to the boundary of land held by 'the people of the horse'. [*kin-**caip**-ul*]

Kincardine (Aberdeenshire, Fife, Highland, Tayside) *Kincardynonele* 1250 (A) *Kyncardyn* 1471–79 (F) 'end of the thicket' from Gaelic *ceann* 'head, end' and Pictish *carrden* 'thicket'. The historical form of Kincardine in Aberdeenshire reflects the full name of Kincardine O'Neil. [*kin-**car**-din*]

Kinghorn (Fife) *Kingorn* 1128 'end of the bog' from Gaelic *ceann* 'head, end' and *gronn* 'bog, marsh'. [***king**-horn*]

Kingussie (Highland) *Kinguscy* c.1210 'head of the pine wood' from Gaelic *ceann* 'head, end' and *giuthsach* 'pine trees'. [*king-**yoos**-ee*]

Kinkell (Fife, Highland) *Kinnakelle* 1199 (F), *Kynkell* 1479 (H) 'end of the wood' from Gaelic *ceann* 'head, end' *na* 'of the' *coille* 'wood'. [*kin-**kell***]

Kinlochleven (Highland) *Kean-Loch-Moir* c.1590, *Kinlochleven* 1750 'the head of the loch of the river Leven' from Gaelic *ceann* 'head, end' and *loch* 'loch, lake', and a river-name from *leamhan* 'elm'. [*kin-loch-**leev**-in*]

Kinnoul (Perth & Kinross) *Kynul* 1250 'the head of the rock' from Gaelic *ceann* 'head, end' and *ail* 'rock, stone'. [*kin-**ool***]

Kinross (Perth & Kinross) *Kynros* c.1144 'end of the promontory' Gaelic *ceann* 'head, end' and *ros* 'promontory, wood'. [*kin-**ross***]

Kintail (Highland) *Kyntale* 1342 'the head of the salt water' from Gaelic *ceann* 'head, end' *an t-* 'of the' *sàil* 'salt-water'. [*kin-**tail***]

Kintore (Aberdeenshire) *Kyntor* 1249–86 'hill end' from Gaelic *ceann* 'head, end' and *tòrr* 'heap, mound, low hill'. [*kin-**toar***]

Kintyre (Argyll & Bute) *Ciunntire* 807, *Kentir* 1128 'end of the land' from Gaelic *ceann* 'head, end' and *tìr* 'land'. [*kin-**tire***]

Kippen (Stirling) *Kippane* 1466 '(place of) the little stump' from Gaelic *ceap* 'stump, block' and the diminutive suffix *–an*. [***kip**-in*]

Kirkbister (Orkney) *Kirkbustir* 1492, **Kirkabister** (Shetland) *Kirkbuster* c.1507–13 'farmstead of the church' from Old Norse *kirkja* 'church' and *bólstaðr* 'dwelling, farmstead'. [***kirk**-biss-ter, **kirk**-a-biss-ter*]

Kirkcaldy (Fife) *Kircaledin* 1240 'place of the hard fort' from Pictish *caer* 'fort, stronghold' *caled* 'hard' and the locative ending *–in* 'place of'. [*kir-**caw**-dee*]

Kirkconnel (Dumfries & Galloway) *Kirconnel* 1296 'St Conall's church' from Old Norse *kirkja* 'church' and the name of the Celtic saint *Conall (Convallus).* [*kir-**con**-ull*]

Kirkcowan (Dumfries & Galloway) *Kirkewane* 1485 'St Eoghan's church' from Old Norse *kirkja* or Scots *kirk* 'church' and the name of the Celtic saint *Eoghan.* [*kir-**cow**-an*]

Kirkcudbright (Dumfries & Galloway) *Kirkcubre* 1511, *Kirkcudbrecht* 1549 'St Cuthbert's church' from Old Norse *kirkja* 'church' and the name of the Northumbrian saint *Cuthbert.* [*kir-**coo**-bree*]

Kirkgunzeon (Dumfries & Galloway) *Cherchwinni* 1159–81, *Kirkewinnen* 1174–99 'St Finnian's church' from Old Norse *kirkja* or Old English *cirice* 'church' and the name of the Celtic saint *Finnian,* in the Brittonic form *Uinniau.* [*kir-**gun**-yin*]

Kirkintilloch (East Dunbartonshire) *Caerpentaloch* 10thC, *Kirkentulach* c.1200 'fort at the end of hillock' from Brittonic *caer* 'fort, stronghold' with Gaelic *ceann* 'head, end' and *tulach* 'hillock, mound'. The historical forms reveal that Gaelic *ceann* has replaced Brittonic *pen* (also meaning 'head, end') and it seems likely that this was originally a wholly Brittonic name which was later Gaelicised. [*kir-kin-**till**-och*]

Kirkoswald (South Ayrshire) *Karcoswald* 1167, *Kierkoswald* 1201 'St Oswald's church' from Old Norse *kirkja* 'church' and the name of the seventh-century Northumbrian king and saint *Oswald*. [***kir**-koz-wold*]

Kirkpatrick (Dumfries & Galloway) *Kirkepatric* 1179 'St Patrick's church' from Old Norse *kirkja* 'church' and the name of the Celtic saint *Patrick*. [*kirk-**pat**-rick*]

Kirkwall (Orkney) *Kirkiuvagr* c.1225 'bay with a church' from Old Norse *kirkja* 'church' and *vágr* 'bay'. The 'church' in question is St Magnus' Cathedral. [***kirk**-wol*]

Kirriemuir (Angus) *Kerimure* 1229 'Mary's quarter' from Gaelic *ceathramh* 'quarter' and *Moir(e)*, a Gaelic form of Mary. [*kir-ee-**myoor***]

Kyleakin (Highland) *Cheules Akin* 1654 'strait of Haakon' from Gaelic *caol(as)* 'strait, sound' and the name of the Norwegian king Haakon IV, who is said to have sailed through the strait in the thirteenth century. [*ky-**lak**-in*]

Kyle of Lochalsh (Highland) *Lochalsche* 1464 'strait of Loch Alsh' from Gaelic *caol(as)* 'strait, sound' and loch-name *Alsh*, perhaps from *aillseach* 'foaming one'. [*kyle-ov-loch-**alsh***]

Kylesku (Highland) *Kyle Scow* 1755 'narrow strait' from Gaelic *caol(as)* 'strait, sound' and *cumhang* 'narrow'. [*kyle-**skyoo***]

Kylestrome (Highland) *Kowil-stron* 1654, *Kylesrome* 1755 'strait of the current' from Gaelic *caol(as)* 'strait, sound' and Old Norse *straumr* 'current, running water'. [*kyle-**stroam***]

Laggan (Highland) *Lagane* 1531 'the little hollow' from Gaelic *lagan* 'little hollow'. [***lag**-an*]

Lairg (Highland) *Larg* 1230 'the shank' from Gaelic *lorg* 'a shank'. [***lairg***]

Lamlash (North Ayrshire) *Helantmlaysche* 14thC, *Lamblasche* 1637 'Isle of MoLaise' from Gaelic *eilean* 'island' and the name of an Irish monk *Lais* or *Laisren*, with *mo* 'my' added to form *Molaise*. Over the years *Eilean Mo Laise* has been corrupted to the current form of Lamlash. The name originally referred to Holy Island in Lamlash Bay. [*lam-**lash***]

Lammermuir (Borders & East Lothian) *Lombormore* c.1050 (B), *Lambremor* 1114 (EL) 'moorland of the lambs' from Old English *lambra* (the genitive plural form of *lamb*) and *mōr* 'moorland'. [***lam**-er-myoor*]

Lanark (South Lanarkshire) *Lannerc* 1187–89 'the glade' from Brittonic *lanerc* 'clearing, glade'. [***lan**-ark*]

Langholm (Dumfries & Galloway) *Langeholme* 1249 'long water meadow' from Old Norse *langr* 'long' and *holmr* 'islet, water meadow'. [***lang**-um*]

Largo (Fife) *Largau* 1140–52, *Largach* 1199 'slope place' from Gaelic *learg* 'slope' with an *-ach* suffix indicating 'place of'. [***lar**-go*]

Largs (North Ayrshire) *Larghes* c.1140 '(place of) the slope' from Gaelic *learg* 'slope' and possibly the Old Gaelic suffix *-es* which indicates 'place of'. [***largz***]

Lasswade (Midlothian) *Laswade* 1148 'pasture ford' from Old English *lǣs* 'pasture, meadowland' (in the possessive form *lǣswe*) and *(ge)wæd* 'ford'. [*lass-**waid***]

Laurencekirk (Aberdeenshire) *Cuneued* 1189–93, *Kirktoun de Conveth alias St Laurence* 1672 'St Laurence's church'. The town was originally known as 'Kirkton of St Laurence', from Scots *kirk* 'church' and *toun* 'farm, settlement', and the name of the English saint, *Laurence of Canterbury*. [***law**-rens-kirk*]

Laxay (Western Isles) *Laxa* 1654 'salmon river' from Old Norse *lax* 'salmon' and *á* 'river'. [***lax**-ay*]

Laxford (Highland) *Laxfuird* 1559 'salmon sea-loch' from Old Norse *lax* 'salmon' and *fjǫrðr* 'fjord, sea-loch'. [***lax**-ford*]

Leaston (East Lothian) *Laysynbi* 1294 'freed man's farm' from Old Norse *leysingi* 'freed man' and Old English *tūn* 'village, farm, estate'. The historical form reveals that *tūn* was sometimes substituted with Old Norse *bœr, býr* 'farm, settlement'. [*lee-stun*]

Legerwood (Borders) *Ledgardeswde* 1127 'Ledgard's wood' from the Middle English personal name *Ledgard* (from Old English *Leodgeard*) and *wudu* 'wood'. [*leh-jerr-wood*]

Leith (Edinburgh) *Inverlet* c.1130, *Inverlethe* c.1315 'mouth of the Leith' from Gaelic *inbhir* 'river mouth, confluence' and a river-name which may derive from Brittonic *llaith* 'damp, moist'. [*leeth*]

Leitholm (Borders) *Letham* 1165–1214 'village on the Leet' from the river-name *Leet*, which is from Old English *(ge)læt* 'water conduit' and *hām* 'homestead, village'. [*leet-um*]

Lendrick (Stirling) *Lennerick* 1669 'the glade' from Brittonic/Pictish *lanerc* 'clearing, glade'. [*len-drick*]

Lennoxtown (East Dunbartonshire) 'Lennox's town'. This eighteenth-century town takes its name from the Earls and Dukes of Lennox, who are named in turn from the ancient territory of Lennox, from Gaelic *leamhanach* 'abounding in elms', from *leamhan* 'elm'. [*len-ux-tun*]

Lenzie (East Dunbartonshire) *Liagne* 1341, *Leigne* 1341 'damp meadow' from Gaelic *lèana* 'swampy plain, meadow'. [*lenn-zee*]

Lerwick (Shetland) *Lerwick* 1625 'mud bay' from Old Norse *leir* 'mud, clay' and *vík* 'bay'. [*ler-wick*]

Lesmahagow (South Lanarkshire) *Lesmahagu* 1144 'garden of my little saint Fechin' from Gaelic *lios* 'garden, enclosure' *mo* 'my' and the name of the Celtic saint *Féchín* in the diminutive form *Fhégu*. [*lez-ma-hay-go*]

Leswalt (Dumfries & Galloway) *Leswalt* c.1275 'grass court' from Brittonic *llys* 'court, hall' and *gwellt* 'pasture, grass'. [*lez-wolt, lez-**wolt***]

Leuchars (Fife) *Lowhcres, Loheres* 1173–78, *Lochres* 1183–87 'place of rushes' from Gaelic *luachar* 'reeds, rushes' and the Old Gaelic suffix *–es* which indicates 'place of'. [***looch**-urz*]

Leurbost (Western Isles) *Duyrbost* 1662, *Leurbost* 1776 perhaps 'mud farm' from Old Norse *leir* 'mud, clay' and *bólstaðr* 'dwelling, farmstead', although the first historical form throws some doubt on the initial element. [***loor**-bost*]

Lewis (Western Isles) *Leodus* c.1100 This name is obscure. It has been interpreted as 'house of songs' from Old Norse *ljóð* 'song, lay' and *hús* 'house'. An alternative interpretation is 'marshy place' from Gaelic *leoghuis* 'marshy', but it is likely that this is an older pre-Celtic name. [***loo**-iss*]

Linlithgow (West Lothian) *Linlitcu* 1124–47 'lake in the moist hollow' from Brittonic *llyn* 'lake' *llaith* 'damp, moist' and *cau* 'hollow'. [*lin-**lith**-go*]

Lionel (Western Isles) *Lionel* 1820 'flax field' from Old Norse *lín* 'flax' and *völlr* 'field'. [***lyn**-il*]

Lismore (Argyll & Bute) *Lesmor* 1249 'big garden' from Gaelic *lios* 'garden, enclosure' and *mòr* 'big'. [*lis-**moar***]

Livingston (West Lothian) *Uilla Leuing* 1124–52, *Leuiggestun* 1153–65 'Leving's farmstead' from the Middle English personal name *Leving* and *toun* 'village, farm, estate'. [***liv**-ing-stun*]

Loanhead (Midlothian) *Loneheid* 1618 'end of the lane' from Scots *loan* 'lane, path giving access to grazing land' and *heid* 'head, end'. [*loan-**hedd***]

Lochawe (Argyll & Bute) *Lochaw* 1450, *Lochhow* 1540–41 'loch of the river Awe' from Gaelic *loch* 'lake, sea-inlet' and the river name *Awe* derived from *abh* 'stream, river'. [*loch-**awe***]

Loch Broom (Highland) *Lochbraon* 1227, *Loghbren* 1275 'loch of the river Broom' from Gaelic *loch* 'lake, sea-inlet' and the river name Broom, from *braon* 'drop, shower, water'. [*loch-**broom***]

Loch Carron (Highland) *Loghcarn* 1275, *Lochcarryn* 1474 'loch of the river Carron' from Gaelic *loch* 'lake, sea-inlet' and the river name Carron, from pre-Celtic **karona* which derives from the root **kar-* 'hard, stone, stony'. [*loch-**carr**-un*]

Loch Duntelchaig (Highland) *L. Duntelchah* 1789 'loch of Duntelchaig' from Gaelic *loch* 'loch, sea-inlet' and the place-name Duntelchaig, which is from Gaelic *dùn* 'fortified place' and *seilcheag* 'snail', in reference to the snail-shaped hill above the loch. [*loch-dun-**telch**-aig*]

Lochgelly (Fife) *Lochgelly* 1290–96 'loch of the shining water' from Gaelic *loch* 'lake, sea-inlet' and *geallaidh* 'shining'. [*loch-**gell**-ay*]

Lochgilphead (Argyll & Bute) *Louchgilp* a.1246, *Lochgilpshead* 1650 'the end of the chisel-shaped loch' from Gaelic *loch* 'lake, sea-inlet' and *gilb* 'chisel', to which Scots *head* 'head, end' was subsequently added. [*loch-**gil**-ped*]

Lochindorb (Moray) *Lochindorb* 1789 perhaps 'loch of the minnows' from Gaelic *loch* 'lake, sea-inlet' *nan* 'of the' *doirb* 'minnow(s)'. [*loch-in-**dorb***]

Lochinver (Highland) *Loch Inver* 1750 'loch at the river mouth' from Gaelic *loch* 'lake, sea-inlet' and *inbhir* 'river mouth, confluence'. [*loch-**in**-ver*]

Loch Lomond (Stirling) *L. Lomnan* a.1200, *L Lomne* c.1225 'loch of (Ben) Lomond' from Gaelic *loch* 'lake, sea-inlet' and *Lomond* from Brittonic/Pictish *llumon* 'a beacon'. The mountain rises up from the eastern shore of the loch. [*loch-**low**-mund*]

Loch Long (Argyll & Bute, Highland) *Loch Loung* 1654 (AB), *Loch Ling* 1820 (H) 'loch of ships' from Gaelic *loch* 'lake, sea-inlet' and *long* 'ship'. [*loch-**long***]

Loch Maben (Dumfries & Galloway) *Locmaban* 1166 perhaps 'loch of Mabon' from Gaelic *loch* 'lake, sea-inlet' and the personal name *Mabon*, from Early Celtic *maponos* 'boy, male child'. [*loch-**may**-bin*]

Loch Ness (Highland) *Nesa* c.700, *Nis* 1300, *Loch Ness* 1654 'loch of the river Ness' from Gaelic *loch* 'lake, sea-inlet' and an obscure Celtic or pre-Celtic river name from the root **ned-* meaning 'wet, to flood'. [*loch-**ness***]

Loch Rannoch (Perth & Kinross) *Lacus de Rannach* 1502 'bracken loch' from Gaelic *loch* 'lake, sea-inlet' and *raineach* 'fern, bracken'. [*loch-**rann**-och*]

Lockerbie (Dumfries & Galloway) *Locardebi* 1194–1214, *Lok(k)ertby* 1510 'Lockhart's settlement' The *Loccard* or *Lockhart* family were an important land-owning family in the twelfth century, giving their name to several places in Scotland. It is possible that this surname replaces an older Scandinavian personal name. See also Stevenston and Symingtoun. [***lock**-er-bee*]

Longniddry (East Lothian) *Nodref* 1315–21, *Langnodryf* 1315–21 '(long) new settlement' from Brittonic *newydd* 'new' and *tref* 'farm, settlement', to which Scots *lang* 'long' was subsequently added. [*long-**nid**-ree*]

Lossiemouth (Moray) *Lossy* 1501 'mouth of the Lossie' from the river-name *Lossie*, derived from Gaelic *lus* 'a plant, a herb'. English *mouth* was added to form the name of the town. [***loss**-ee-mouth*]

Luss (Argyll & Bute) *Lus* 1225 '(place of) plants' from Gaelic *lus* 'a plant, a herb'. [***luss***]

Lybster (Highland) *Libister* 1538 'slope farm' from Old Norse *hlíð* 'slope' and *bólstaðr* 'dwelling, farmstead'. [***libe**-ster*]

Macduff (Aberdeenshire) This eighteenth-century name was given by James Duff, second Earl of Fife, in honour of his father William Duff. The older Gaelic name was Doune. [*mack-**duff***]

Machrihanish (Argyll & Bute) *Macharhanys* 1481 'the plain of Sanas' from Gaelic *machair* 'fertile coastal plain' and obscure district name *Sanas*, which might refer to a type of grass or plant. [*mach-ri-**han**-ish*]

Mallaig (Highland) *Malag* 1820 perhaps 'gull bay' from Old Norse *már* 'seagull' and *vík* 'bay'. [***ma**-laig*]

Markinch (Fife) *Marckinch* c.1028–55 'horse meadow' from Gaelic *marc* 'horse' and *innis* 'island, raised meadow'. [*mark-**insh***]

Maryculter (Aberdeen) *Marecultir* 1548 'the back-land of St Mary' from an existing place-name containing Gaelic *cùl* 'back' and *tìr* 'land' and the name of saint *Mary*. The church is dedicated to St Mary, and this dedication was added to the name to distinguish it from nearby Peterculter. [*may-ree-**coo**-ter*]

Mauchline (East Ayrshire) *Machline* c.1130 'plain by the pool' from Gaelic *magh* 'plain, field' and *linn* 'pool, pond'. [***moch**-lin*]

Maybole (South Ayrshire) *Meibothel* c.1180. 'maiden's dwelling' from Old English *mǣge* 'maiden, kinswoman' and *bōðl* 'house, dwelling'. [***may**-boal*]

Melbost (Western Isles) *Naeglabost* 1662, *Melbust* 1776 'grassy-sandbank farm' from Old Norse *melr* 'grassy-sandbank' and *bólstaðr* 'dwelling, farmstead'. [***mel**-bost*]

Melness (Highland) *Melness* 1379 'grassy-sandbank headland' from Old Norse *melr* 'grassy-sandbank' and *nes* 'headland'. [***mel**-ness*]

Melrose (Borders) *Mailros* c.700 'bare moor' from Brittonic *moel* 'bare, bald' and *rhos* 'moor, promontory'. [***mel**-rose*]

Melvaig (Highland) *Malefage* 1566, *Melvaick* c.1660–70, **Melvich** (Highland) *Mealloch* la16thC, *Melvich* 1750 'grassy-sandbank bay' from Old Norse *melr* 'grassy-sandbank' and *vík* 'bay'. [***mel**-vig, **mel**-vich*]

Menstrie (Clackmannanshire) *Mestryn* 1261, *Mestreth* 1263 'settlement on the plain' from Brittonic *maes* 'plain, open land' and *tref* 'farm, settlement'. [***men**-stree*]

Methil (Fife) *Methkil* 1207 'middle church' from Gaelic *meadh(on)* 'middle' and *cill* 'church'. [***meth**-il*]

Middlebie (Dumfries & Galloway) *Middiby* 1291, *Middelby* 1296 'the middle farm' from Old English *middel* 'middle' and Old Norse *bœr, býr* 'farm, settlement'. [***mid**-il-bee*]

Minnigaff (Dumfries & Galloway) *Monygof* 1471 'moor of the smith' from Brittonic *mynydd* 'moor, mountain' *y* 'of the' *gof* 'smith'. [*minn-ee-**gaff***]

Moffat (Dumfries & Galloway) *Moffet* 1179 possibly 'the long plain' from Gaelic *magh* 'plain, field' and *fada* long'. [***moff**-at*]

Montrose (Angus) *Munros* c.1178 'moor of the promontory' from Gaelic *mon* (a shortened form of *monadh*) 'moor' and *ros* 'point, promontory'. [*mon-**trose***]

Moray (Moray) *Moreb* c.970, *Morref* c.1295 'sea(board) settlement' from early Celtic *mori* 'sea' and *treb* 'settlement'. This ancient province also gives its name to a modern unitary authority and to the Moray Firth. [***murr**-ay*]

Morebattle (Borders) *Mereboda* c.1124, *Merbotl* 1165–92 'lake dwelling' from Old English *mere* 'pond, lake' and *bōðl* 'house, dwelling'. [***moar**-bat-il*]

Motherwell (North Lanarkshire) *Matervelle* a.1250, *Moydirwal* 1265 'source of the spring' from Scots *moder* 'fountainhead, source (of water)' and *well* 'spring, pool'. [***muth**-er-well*]

Moulinearn (Perth & Kinross) *Mulinearn* 1820 perhaps 'bare hill of the alders' from Gaelic *maoilinn* 'bare hill' and *fheàrna* (from *feàrna*) 'alder tree'. [*mool-in-**ern***]

Moy (Highland) *Muy* c.1235 'the plain' from Gaelic *magh* 'plain, field'. [***moy***]

Muck (Highland) *Helantmok* 1370 'isle of pigs' from Gaelic *eilean* 'island' *nam* 'of the' *muc* 'pigs, swine'. The island is now known simply as *Muck*. [***muck***]

Munlochy (Highland) *Munlochy* 1328 '(place) at the foot of the loch' from the Gaelic *bun* 'foot, bottom' and *loch* 'loch, lake'. [*mun-**loch**-ee*]

Musselburgh (East Lothian) *Muselburge* c.1100 'mussel town' from Old English *mus(c)le* 'mussel, shellfish' and *burh* 'fortified place'. [***muss**-il-burr-a*]

Nairn (Highland) *Inuernaren* c.1195 '(mouth of) the river Nairn' from Gaelic *inbhir* 'river mouth, confluence' and the pre-Celtic river name *Narunn*, from the root **ner*- 'dive, cave, submerge'. [***nairn***]

New Aberdour (Aberdeenshire) *Aberdouer* 1178–99 'mouth of the Dour' from Pictish *aber* 'river mouth' and the Dour Burn. The burn name is from *duvr*, a Pictish word for water, which was later Gaelicised as *dobhar*. The village of New Aberdour was founded in 1798, with '*New*' being prefixed to the old parish name to distinguish it from an older hamlet. [***new**-ab-er-dowr*]

Newbattle (Midlothian) *Neubotle* 1140 'new dwelling' from Old English *nīwe* 'new' and *bōðl* 'house, dwelling'. [***new**-bat-il*]

Newton Mearns (Renfrewshire) *Newtoun de Mernis* 1609 'the new town in the parish of Mearns'. *Mearns* is from Gaelic *An Mhaoirne* 'the Stewartry', referring to an area which was administered by a steward. [*new-tun-**mairns***]

Newton Stewart (Dumfries & Galloway) This 'new town of Stewart' was laid out in 1677 by William Stewart, son of the second Earl of Galloway. [*new-tun-**styoo**-art*]

Niddrie (Edinburgh, West Lothian) *Nudreth* 1140, *Nodrif* 1166–1214 (E) *Nudreff* 1370 (WL) 'new settlement' from Brittonic *newydd* 'new' and *tref* 'farm, settlement'. [***nid**-ree*]

North Berwick (East Lothian) *Beruvik* c.1225, *Northberwyk* 1250 '(northern) barley farm' from Old English *bere* 'barley' and *wīc* 'farm, settlement'. 'North' was subsequently added to the name to distinguish it from Berwick-upon-Tweed in England. [*north-**berr**-ick*]

Oban (Argyll & Bute) *Oban* 1643 'the little bay' from Gaelic *òban* 'small bay'. The modern Gaelic form is *An t-Òban Latharnach* 'the little bay of Lorne'. [***oa**-ban*]

Ochil Hills (Perth & Kinross) *Oychellis* 1461 'high hills' from Brittonic/Pictish *uchel* 'high'. [***oach**-il-hillz*]

Ochiltree (East Ayrshire, West Lothian) *Uchiltrie* 1406 (EA), *Ockiltre* 1211–14 (WL) 'high settlement' from Brittonic *uchel* 'high' and *tref* 'farm, settlement'. [***oach**-il-tree*]

Old Kilpatrick (West Dunbartonshire) *Kilpatrik* a.1199, *Wester Kilpatrik* 1580, *Old Killpatrick* 1755 'older church of St Patrick' from Gaelic *cill* 'church' and the name of the Celtic saint *Patrick*, to which first *West* and then *Old* were prefixed, to distinguish the village from *East* or *New Kilpatrick* (modern Bearsden) when the parish was divided in half in the mid-seventeenth century. [*old-kil-**pat**-rick*]

Orkney (Orkney) *Orkaneya* 970 perhaps 'seal island' from Old Norse *orkn* 'seal' and *ey* 'island', a reshaping of an existing Celtic place-name referring to the *Orc* tribe, whose name many have meant 'boar' or 'pig' people. [***ork**-nay*]

Ormiston (Borders, East Lothian) *Hormiston* 1214–49 (B), *Ormeston* 1628 (EL) 'Orm's farm' from the Old Norse personal name *Ormr* and Old English *tūn* 'village, farm, estate' or Scots *toun* 'farm, settlement'. [***or**-mis-tin*]

Oxnam (Borders) *Oxenham* 1165–1214 'village of the oxen' from the genitive plural of Old English *oxa* 'oxen' and *hām* 'homestead, village'. [***ox**-nam*]

Pabanish (Western Isles) 'priest headland' from Old Norse *papi* 'priest' and *nes* 'headland'. [***pa**-ba-nish*]

Pabay, Pabbay (Western Isles) *Paba* 1580, *Paba* 1654 (both) 'priest island' from Old Norse *papi* 'priest' and *ey* 'island'. [***pa**-bay*]

Paisley (Renfrewshire) *Passelek* 1296 'major church' from Brittonic *passeleg* 'major church', a loanword from Latin *basilica.* [***payz**-lee*]

Papadil (Highland) 'priest valley' from Old Norse *papi* 'priest' and *dalr* 'valley'. [***pap**-a-dill*]

Papa Stour (Shetland) *Papey Stora* 1229 '(great) priest island' from Old Norse *papi* 'priest' *ey* 'island' and *stórr* 'big, great'. [*pa-pa-**stoor***]

Peebles (Borders) *Pobles* c.1124, *Pebles* c.1126 'place of temporary shelters' from Brittonic *pebyll* 'tents, pavilions', possibly in the sense of summer shielings. [***pee**-bils*]

Penicuik (Midlothian) *Penikok* 1250 'hill of the cuckoo' from Brittonic *penn* 'head, end', *y* 'of the' *cog* 'cuckoo'. [***pen**-ee-cook*]

Perth (Perth & Kinross) *Pert* c.1128, *St Johnstoun or Perth* 1220 '(place at the) thicket' from Pictish *pert* 'copse, thicket, hedge'. Perth had the alternative name of *St Johnstoun* during the medieval period, reflecting the importance of the parish church dedicated to St John the Baptist. [***perth***]

Peterculter (Aberdeenshire) *Cultir* 1178–1199, *Petirculter* 1526 'the back-land of St Peter' from an existing place-name containing Gaelic *cùl* 'back' and *tìr* 'land' and the name of saint *Peter*. The church is dedicated to St Peter, and this dedication was added to the name to distinguish it from nearby Maryculter. [*pee-ter-**coo**-ter*]

Peterhead (Aberdeenshire) *Inuerugy Petri* 1287, *Petyrheid* 1544 'Peter's headland'. The town takes its name from a church on the headland which was dedicated to St Peter. The older Gaelic name was Inverugie. [*pee-ter-**hedd***]

Pitbladdo (Fife) *Petblatho* 1481, *Petblado* 1494 'the meal land-holding' from Gaelic *pett* 'land-holding, unit of land' and Pictish *blawd* or Gaelic *blàth* 'meal, flour'. [*pit-**bladd**-o*]

Pitcairn (Fife) *Petcarn* 1250 'the land-holding of the cairn' from Gaelic *pett* 'land-holding, unit of land' and *càrn* 'cairn, heap of stones'. [*pit-**cairn***]

Pitcaple (Aberdeenshire) *Petcapyle* c.1438 'the horse land-holding' from Gaelic *pett* 'land-holding, unit of land' and *capall* 'horse, mare'. [*pit-**kay**-pill*]

Pitcroy (Moray) *Pitcroy* 1661 'hard land-holding' from Gaelic *pett* 'land-holding, unit of land'and *cruaidh* 'hard, firm'. [*pit-**croy***]

Pitkerro (Angus) *Pitcarrow* 1524 'the quarter land-holding' from Gaelic *pett* 'land-holding, unit of land' and *ceathramh* 'a quarter'. [*pit-**kerr**-o*]

Pitliver (Fife) *Lauer* 1128, *Petliuer* 1227 'the book land-holding' from Gaelic *pett* 'land-holding, unit of land' and *leabhar* 'book'. The name may refer to the lands of a church which held a special copy of the Gospels. [*pit-**liv**-ir*]

Pitlochry (Perth & Kinross) *Pitlochrie* 1581 'the land-holding of the stony place' from Gaelic *pett* 'land-holding, unit of land' and *cloichreach* 'stones, stony place'. [*pit-**loch**-ree*]

Pitlurg (Aberdeenshire) *Petnalurge* 1232 'land-holding of the shank' from Gaelic *pett* 'land-holding, unit of land' *na* 'of the' *lorg* 'shank'. [*pit-**lurg***]

Pitmedden (Aberdeenshire) *Petmeddane* 1532 'the middle land-holding' from Gaelic *pett* 'land-holding, unit of land' and *meadhon* 'middle'. [*pit-**med**-in*]

Pitsligo (Aberdeenshire) *Petslegach* 1426 'shelly land-holding' from Gaelic *pett* 'land-holding, unit of land' and *sligeach* 'shelly'. [*pit-**sly**-go*]

Pittencrieff (Fife) *Pethincreff* 1291 'the land-holding of the tree' from Gaelic *pett* 'land-holding, unit of land' *nan* 'of the' *craobh* 'tree'. [*pit-in-**kreef***]

Pittendreich (Fife, Moray) *Pettendrech* c.1212–16 (F), *Petendrech* 1238 (M) 'the land-holding of the (good) aspect' from Gaelic *pett* 'land-holding, unit of land' *an* 'of the' and *dreach* 'aspect, face, hill-slope'. [*pit-in-**dreech***]

Pittenweem (Fife) *Petnewem* 1140–45 'the land-holding of the cave' from Gaelic *pett* 'land-holding, unit of land' *na h-* 'of the' *uaimh* 'cave'. [*pit-in-**weem***]

Plockton (Highland) *Plock* 1679, *Plockton* 1820 'town of the lump' from Gaelic *ploc* 'lump, pimple', to which Scots *toun* 'farm, settlement' was added. The Gaelic name is *Am Ploc* 'the lump' or *Ploc Loch Aillse* 'the lump of Lochalsh'. [***plock**-tun*]

Pluscarden (Moray) *Ploschardin* 1124, *Pluscardyn* 1226 'place of the thicket' from Pictish *plas* 'place' and *carrden* 'thicket'. [***pluss**-cardin*]

Polmont (Falkirk) *Polmunth* 1319 perhaps 'pool hill' from Gaelic *poll* 'pool, pit, hollow' and *monadh* 'mountain, hill, moor'. [***poal**-mont*]

Portban (Argyll & Bute) 'white harbour' from Gaelic *port* 'harbour, ferry' and *bàn* 'white, fair'. [*port-**baan***]

Port Charlotte (Argyll & Bute) This village name commemorates the mother of Walter Frederick Campbell of Islay. [*port-**shar**-lot*]

Port Ellen (Argyll & Bute) This village name commemorates Lady Eleanor (Ellen) Campbell, wife of Walter Frederick Campbell of Islay. [*poar-**tell**-in*]

Portessie (Moray) *Rottinslough* 1594, *Portessie* 1870 'port of the waterfall' from Gaelic *port* 'harbour, ferry' and *easa* or *easaidh* from *eas* 'waterfall, rapids'. The older name of the village was *Rottinslough*. [*poar-**tess**-ee*]

Portgordon (Moray) This village was founded in the late eighteenth-century by Alexander, fourth Duke of Gordon. [*port-**gord**-in*]

Portincaple (Argyll & Bute) *Portinchapil* a.1350, *Portincable* 1395 'port of the horse(s)' from Gaelic *port* 'harbour, ferry', *nan* 'of the' *capall* 'horse, mare'. [*port-in-**kay**-pill*]

Portknockie (Moray) *Portknocky* 1741 perhaps 'harbour at the hilly place' from Gaelic *port* 'harbour, ferry' and *cnocaidh* 'hilly place' from *cnoc* 'round hill, knoll'. [*port-**nock**-ee*]

Portmahomack (Highland) *Portmachalmok* 1678 'port of my little St Colman' from Gaelic *port* 'harbour, ferry' *mo* 'my' and the name of the Celtic saint *Colmán*, in the diminutive form *Colmag*. [*port-ma-**homm**-uck*]

Portobello (Edinburgh) This name is from a local house, built by a sailor who claimed to have been at the capture of Porto Bello in Panama in 1739. The original name of the village was Figgate. [*port-o-**bell**-o*]

Portpatrick (Dumfries & Galloway) *Portpatrick* 1653 'harbour of St Patrick' from Gaelic *port* 'harbour, ferry' and the name of the Celtic saint *Patrick*. [*port-**pat**-rick*]

Portree (Highland) *Portri* 1549 The modern Gaelic form of this name is *Port Rìgh* 'king's harbour', from *port* 'harbour, ferry' and *rìgh* 'king', and is said to refer to a visit made by King James V in the sixteenth century. However, the name originally contained the word *ruighe* 'slope', with the meaning 'harbour at the slope'. [*poar-**tree***]

Portsoy (Aberdeenshire) *Portsoy* 1649 perhaps 'port of the saithe' from Gaelic *port* 'harbour, ferry' and *saoithe* 'saithe, pollock'. [*port-**soy***]

Prestonpans (East Lothian) *Saltprestoun* 1587 '(salt) pans of the priest(s)' farm' from Old English *prēost* 'priest' or *prēosta* 'priests' and *tūn* 'village, farm, estate', to which Scots *pans* was later added to refer to the salt-works here. [*press-tun-**pans***]

Prestwick (South Ayrshire) *Prestwic* 1165–73 'farm of the priest(s)' from Old English *prēost* 'priest' or *prēosta* 'priests' and *wīc* 'farm, settlement'. [***prest**-wick*]

Queensferry (Edinburgh, Fife) *Qwenys-ferry* c.1420 (F) These names mark the historical crossing points of the ferry over the Firth of Forth. The queen in question is St Margaret, wife of Malcolm Canmore. North Queensferry is at the Fife end of the crossing, and South Queensferry is on the Edinburgh side. The ferry was replaced in 1964 by the Forth Road Bridge. [***kweenz**-fur-ay*]

Rattray (Perth & Kinross) *Rotrefe* 1291 'farm by the fort' from Gaelic or Pictish *ràth* 'fort' and Pictish *tref* 'farm, settlement'. [***rat**-ray*]

Redkirk (Dumfries & Galloway) *Red kirke* 1552, *Ryidkirk* 1660 'red church' from Old English *rēad* 'red' and Old Norse *kirkja* 'church' or Scots *kirk*, probably replacing the Old English cognate *cirice*. 'Red' here may refer to the local sandstone. [***red**-kirk*]

Renfrew (Renfrewshire) *Reinfry* c.1128 'point of the current' from Brittonic *rhyn* 'point, promontory' and *frwd* 'torrent, current'. [***ren**-froo*]

Renton (West Dunbartonshire) This eighteenth-century name commemorates Cecilia Renton, who was married to a nephew of local novelist Tobias Smollett. [***ren**-tun*]

Reston (Borders) *Riston* 1095–1100 'brushwood farm' from Old English *hrīs* 'brushwood, shrubs' and *tūn* 'village, farm, estate'. [***res**-tun*]

Rhu (Argyll & Bute) *Row* 1750 'the headland' from Gaelic *rubha* 'headland, point'. [***roo***]

Riccarton (Borders, East Ayrshire) *Ricardeston* 1296 (B), *Ricardten* 1208 (EA) 'Richard's farm' from the Old English personal name *Richærd* and *tūn* 'village, farm, estate'. [*rick-ar-tun*]

Rosehearty (Aberdeenshire) *Rossawarty* 1508 'Abhartach's point' from Gaelic *ros* 'point, promontory' and the Celtic personal name *Abhartach*. [*roaz-**har**-tay*]

Rosemarkie (Highland) *Rosmarkensis* c.1128, *Rosmarky* 1510 perhaps 'headland of the Marky' from Gaelic *ros* 'point, promontory' and a stream-name derived from *marc* 'horse'. [*roaz-**mar**-kee*]

Ross (Highland) *Rossia* a.1100 This historical county name may be either from Gaelic *ros* 'point, promontory' or from the related Pictish *ros* 'moorland'. [***ross***]

Rosyth (Fife) *Rossiue* 1162–64 'headland of Fife' from Gaelic *ros* 'point, promontory' and the possessive form of *Fíb* 'Fife'. [*raw-**syth***]

Rothes (Moray) *Rothes* 1238 'fortified place' from Gaelic *ràth* 'fort' or a Pictish cognate **roth*. [***roth**-is*]

Rothesay (Argyll & Bute) *Rothersay* 1321 'Rother's isle' from the personal name *Roderick* (*Ruari*) and Old Norse *ey* 'island'. Roderick was the son of Reginald, to whom the Isle of Bute was granted in the thirteenth century. The Gaelic name is *Baile Bhòid* 'town of Bute'. [***roth**-say*]

Rowardennan (Stirling) *Row Ardenan* 1750 'the point of Adomnan's headland' from Gaelic *rubha* 'headland, point' *àird, àrd* 'height, promontory' and the name of the Gaelic saint *Adomnán*. [*row-ar-**denn**-un*]

Roxburgh (Borders) *Rokesburge* c.1120 'Hroc's fortification' from the Old English personal name *Hrōc* and *burh* 'fortified place'. [***rox**-burr-a*]

Rum (Highland) *Ruim* 677, *Rume* 1292 The meaning of this island name is obscure, but it may be pre-Celtic. [***rum***, locally ***room***]

Saltcoats (North Ayrshire) *Saltcoates* 1548 'salt cotts' from Scots *salt* and *cotts* 'cottages'. The name refers to the buildings that were used in the salt-making industry here. [***sol**-coats*]

Sannox (North Ayrshire) *Sannokes* 1548 'sand bay' from Old Norse *sandr* 'sand' and *vík* 'bay'. The name became Gaelicised as *Sannaig*, and the current form derives from the addition of an English *-s* plural. [***san**-ox*]

Sanquhar (Dumfries & Galloway) *Sanchar* a.1150 'old fort' from Gaelic *sean* 'old' and *cathair* 'fort, seat'. [***san**-kar*]

Sauchieburn (Aberdeenshire, Stirling) 'willow stream' from Scots *sauchie* 'willow' and *burn* 'stream'. [***saw**-chee-burn*]

Scarfskerry (Highland) *Scarskerry* 1750 'sea-rock of the cormorant' from Old Norse *skarfr* 'the green cormorant' and *sker* 'sea-rock'. [***skarf**-skerr-ee*]

Scrabster (Highland) *Skarabolstad* c.1387–1395, *Scrabuster* 1527 'farm of the young gull' from Old Norse *skári* 'a young sea-gull' and *bólstaðr* 'dwelling, farmstead'. [***skrab**-stur*]

Selkirk (Borders) *Selechirche* c.1120 'church by the hall' from Old English *sele* 'hall, manor house' and *cirice* 'church' (later becoming Scots *kirk*). [***sell**-kirk*]

Shader (Western Isles) *Shader* 1654 'the dwelling' from Old Norse *setr* 'dwelling'. [***shadd**-er*]

Shandwick (Highland) *Schandwick* 1577, *Sandwick* 1662 'sand bay' from Old Norse *sandr* 'sand' and *vík* 'bay'. [***shand**-wick*]

Shawbost (Western Isles) *Schaboist* 1662 'sea dwelling' from Old Norse *sjár* 'sea' and *bólstaðr* 'dwelling, farmstead'. [***shaw**-bost*]

Shetland (Shetland) *Haltland* c.1100, *Shetland* 1289 'hilt land' from Old Norse *hjalt* 'hilt' and *land*. This was probably a reshaping of an existing Celtic or pre-Celtic name. [***shet**-land*]

Shieldaig (Highland) *Sheildaick* c.1660–70, *Shildaig* 1750 'herring bay' from Old Norse *sild* 'herring' and *vík* 'bay'. [***sheel**-dig*]

Shotts (North Lanarkshire) *Bertrum Schottis* 1552 'the smallholdings' from Scots *s(c)hott* 'portion of land, smallholding'. The historical form reveals that the name previously incorporated a qualifying element which may have been a personal name or surname. [***shotts***]

Skaill (Highland, Orkney) *Scalle* 1492 (O), *Skaill* 1552–53 (H) 'the hall' from Old Norse *skáli* 'hall, hut, shieling'. [***skail***]

Skelbo (Highland) *Scelbo* c.1210, *Scellebol* a.1300 'shell farm' from Old Norse *skel* 'shell' and *ból* 'farm'. [***skel**-bo*]

Skibo (Highland) *Scitheboll* 1230 'Skithi's farm' or 'ship farm' from the Old Norse personal name *Skiði* or the word *skeið* 'long-ship' and *ból* 'farm'. [***skee**-bo*]

Skirza (Highland) *Skersarie* 1635 'Skerrir's shieling' from the Old Norse personal name *Skerrir* and *ǽrgi* 'shieling, summer pasture'. [***skir**-sa*]

Skye (Highland) *Skitis* c.150, *Sceth* 668, *Scia* c.700 This name is uncertain. Possible explanations include 'winged (isle)' from Gaelic *sgiath* 'wing' on the basis of the island's shape, or 'divided (isle)' from Gaelic *sgian* 'knife' again on the basis of Skye's 'knifed' or 'divided' shape. However, the name is more likely to be pre-Celtic in origin. [***sky***]

Slamannan (Falkirk) *Slefmanyn* 1275 'moor of Manau' from Gaelic *sliabh* 'mountain, moorland' and the Brittonic district name *Manau* meaning 'projecting or high land'. [*sla-**man**-an*]

Smailholm (Borders) *Smalham(e)* c.1160, **Smallholm** (Dumfries & Galloway) *Smalham* 1304 'small village' from Old English *smæl* 'small' and *hām* 'homestead, village'. [***smail**-hoam, **small**-hoam*]

Smeaton (Midlothian) *Smithetun* 1124–53, *Smithebi* 1153–65 'smith's town' from Old English *smiþ* or Old Norse *smiþr* 'smith' and Old English *tūn* 'village, farm, estate'. The historical forms reveal that *tūn* was sometimes substituted with Old Norse *bœr, býr* 'farm, settlement'. [***smee**-tun*]

Smerby (Argyll & Bute) *Smerby* 1654 'dairy farm' from Old Norse *smjör* 'butter, dairy produce' and *bœr, býr* 'farm, settlement'. [***smer**-bee*]

Sorbie (Dumfries & Galloway) *Sowreby* 1349 (Dmf), *Sowrby* 1185–1200 (Gal) 'mud settlement' from Old Norse *saurr* 'mud, swamp, mudflats' and *bœr, býr* 'farm, settlement'. [***sor**-bee*]

Soroba (Argyll & Bute) *Sorropa* 1506–07 'mud settlement' from Old Norse *saurr* 'mud, swamp, mudflats' and *bœr, býr* 'farm, settlement'. [***sor**-o-ba*]

St Andrews (Fife) *Sancti Andree* c.1158 '(shrine of) Saint Andrew'. The relics of Scotland's patron saint are said to have been brought to St Andrews in the eighth century. [*sin-**tan**-drooz*]

St Cyrus (Angus) *Ecclesgreig* 1243, *St Sirus* 1750 '(church of) Saint Cyricius'. The older Gaelic form was *Ecclesgreig*, from *eaglais* 'church' and the name *Cyricius* in the form *Girg* or *Girig*. [*sint-**sy**-rus*]

Stemster (Highland) *Stambuster* 1581 'stone farmstead' from Old Norse *steinn* 'stone' and *bólstaðr* 'dwelling, farmstead'. [***stem**-ster*]

Stenhousemuir (Falkirk) *Stan house* c.1200 'moorland by the stone house' from Old English *stān* 'stone' and *hūs* 'house' with the later addition of Scots *muir* 'moorland'. [*sten-hows-**myoor***]

Stevenston (North Ayrshire) *Stevenstoun* 1246 'Steven's farm' from the personal name *Steven* and Scots *toun* 'farm, settlement'. The name commemorates *Stephen Loccard* or *Lockhart*, an important local landowner who is mentioned in several twelfth-century charters.

He is likely to have been related to the *Simon Loccard* commemorated in the various Symington names. See also Lockerbie. [***steev**-inz-tun*]

Stewarton (East Ayrshire) *Stewartoun* 1201 'Steward's estate' from Walter *Seneschal* (High Steward), who owned the estate in the twelfth century. [***stew**-ar-tun*]

Stirling (Stirling) *Strevelin* 1124, *Struelin* c.1125, *Estriuelin* c.1250 This name is obscure. Possible explanations include 'enclosure by the stream' from Gaelic *sruth* 'stream' and *lann* 'enclosed land', or 'dwelling of Melyn' from Brittonic *ystre* 'dwelling' and a personal name *Melyn*. However, the name may be a much older river-name, referring to the river Forth on which Stirling stands. [***stir**-ling*]

Stonehaven (Aberdeenshire) *Stanehiffe* 1506 'stone harbour' from Scots *stane* 'stone' and *hythe* 'harbour, haven, landing place'. Scots *hythe* was later replaced with English *haven*. [*stoan-**hay**-ven*, locally *steen-**hive***]

Stoneykirk (Dumfries & Galloway) *Stanacra* c.1275 'stony land' from Old English *stān* 'stone' and *æcer* 'plot of arable land'. [***stoan**-ee-kirk*, locally ***steen**-ee-kirk*]

Stornoway (Western Isles) *Stornochway* 1511 'steering bay' from Old Norse *stjórnar*, the genitive form of *stjórn* 'steerage, steering' and *vágr* 'bay'. [***stor**-na-way*]

Straiton (Midlothian, South Ayrshire) *Stratone* 1296 (M), *Straton* 1225 (SA) 'village on a Roman road' from Old English *strǣt* 'paved (Roman) road' and *tūn* 'village, farm, estate'. [***stray**-tin*]

Stranraer (Dumfries & Galloway) *Stranrever* c.1320 'the thick promontory' from Gaelic *sròn* 'nose, point, promontory' and *reamhar* 'fat, thick'. [*stran-**raar***]

Strathan (Highland) 'the little valley' from Gaelic *srath* 'broad valley' and the diminutive suffix *–an*. [***stran***]

Strathaven (South Lanarkshire) *Strathouren* c.1190 'broad valley of the Avon Water' from Gaelic *srath* 'broad valley' and the river name *Avon*, which simply means 'river'. [***stray**-vin*]

Strathmiglo (Fife) *Stradmiggloch* 1160–62 'broad valley of Miglo' from Gaelic *srath* 'broad valley' and the existing place-name *Miglo*, meaning 'bog-loch' from either Gaelic or Pictish *mig* 'bog' and Gaelic *loch* 'lake'. [*stra-**mig**-lo*]

Strathnaver (Highland) *Strathnauir* 1268 'broad valley of the river Naver' from Gaelic *srath* 'broad valley' and the river name *Naver* from the pre-Celtic root **nebh-* 'moist, water, mist'. [*strath-**nay**-ver*]

Strathpeffer (Highland) *Strathpefir* 1350 'broad valley of the river Peffer' from Gaelic *srath* 'broad valley' and the river name *Peffer* from Pictich *pevr* 'bright, beautiful'. [*strath-**peff**-er*]

Stroma (Highland) *Straumey* 12thC 'current island' from Old Norse *straumr* 'current, running water' and *ey* 'island'. [***stroa**-ma*]

Stromeferry (Highland) *Strom* 1662, *Strome* 1679 'ferry at Strome' from an existing place-name *Strome* meaning '(place of) the strong current' from Old Norse *straumr* 'current, running water' to which Scots *ferry* was later added. [*stroam-**ferr**-ay*]

Stromness (Orkney) *Stromnesse* 1483 'headland of the (strong) current' from Old Norse *straumr* 'current, running water' and *nes* 'headland'. [***strom**-ness*]

Sullom Voe (Shetland) *Sollom* 1507 'bay of the sunny farm' from Old Norse *sól* 'sun' *heimr* 'home, dwelling' and *vágr* 'bay'. [*sull-um-**voe***]

Sutherland (Highland) *Suthernelande* c.1250 'southern land' from Old Norse *suðr* 'south' and *land* 'land'. Although Sutherland is in the north of Scotland, it was at the southern edge of the Norse territories in Scotland. [***suh**-ther-land*]

Swordale (Highland) *Swerdel, Swerisdale* 1275 'grass valley' from Old Norse *svörðr* 'grass, turf' and *dalr* 'valley'. [***sor**-dail*]

Symington (Borders, South Ayrshire, South Lanarkshire) *Terram Simonis Loccardi* 1160, *Symondstona* 1293 (SA), *Villa Symonis Lockard* c.1189 (SL) 'Simon's settlement' from the personal name *Simon* and Scots *toun* 'farm, settlement'. The Lockhart family held extensive lands across southern Scotland in the twelfth century. See also Stevenston and Lockerbie. [***sy**-ming-tun*]

Tain (Highland) *Tene* 1227, *Thane* 1483 This name originally referred to the River Tain, meaning either 'water, river' from a pre-Celtic root, or 'flowing one' from an Indo-European root **ta, tə-* 'to dissolve, to flow'. The Gaelic name is *Baile Dhubhthaich*, containing Gaelic *baile* 'farm, settlement' and the name of the Celtic saint *Duthac*. [***tain***]

Tarbet, Tarbert (Argyll & Bute, Highland, Western Isles) *Tarbart* 1326 (AB), *Tharberth* 1257 (H), *Terbat* 1654 (WI) 'isthmus, portage' from Gaelic *tairbeart* 'isthmus, narrow neck of land across which boats may be dragged'. [***tar**-bet, **tar**-bert*]

Taynuilt (Argyll & Bute) *Taynuil* 1820 'house by the stream' from Gaelic *taigh* 'house' *an* 'of the' *uillt* (from *allt*) 'burn, stream'. [*tay-**nilt***]

Tayport (Fife) 'port on the river Tay' from the river-name *Tay* which could be a Celtic name meaning 'silent one' or else pre-Celtic **ta-, tə-* 'flowing one' (see **Tain** above) to which Scots *port* was later added. Older names for Tayport include *Portincraig* from Gaelic *port* 'harbour, ferry', *na* 'of the' *creige* (from *creag*) 'rock, crag' and Scots names *Scotscraig* and *Southferry*. [***tay**-port*]

Terregles (Dumfries & Galloway) *Traveregles* c.1275 'settlement of the church' from Brittonic *tref* 'farm, settlement' *yr* 'of the' *eglwys* 'church'. [*tir-**eag**-ilz*]

Threave (Dumfries & Galloway) *Treif* 1422 'the settlement' from Brittonic *tref* 'farm, settlement'. [*threev*]

Thrumster (Highland) *Thrumbister* 1541 'border-land farm' from Old Norse *þruma* 'border-land, outskirts' and *bólstaðr* 'dwelling, farmstead'. [***thrum**-ster*]

Thurso (Highland) *Þórsá* c.1200, *Turseham* c.1200, *Turishau* 1287 'bull's river' from Old Norse *þjórr* 'bull' and *á* 'river'. The historical forms suggest that the original generic may have been Old Norse *haugr* 'cairn, mound'. [***thur**-zoh*]

Tillicoultry (Clackmannanshire) *Tulycultri* 1195, *Tullicultre* c.1199 'hill at the back-land' from Gaelic *tulach* 'knoll, hillock' and a compound containing *cùl* 'back' and *tìr* 'land'. [*til-ee-**coot**-ree*]

Tillyfourie (Aberdeenshire) *Tullochourie* 1628 'hillock of the pasture place' from Gaelic *tulach* 'knoll, hillock' and *phùiridh* 'pasture place' from *pòr* 'pasture, crops'. [*til-ee-**foor**-ee*]

Tinwald (Dumfries & Galloway) *Tynwald* 1335–36

Tingwall (Orkney, Shetland) *Þingavǫll* c.1225 (O), *Þinga velle* 1307 (S) 'assembly field' from Old Norse *þing* 'assembly place, parliament' and *vǫllr* 'field, level ground'. [***tin**-auld, **ting**-wall*]

Tiree (Argyll & Bute) *Tirieth* 12thC, *Tiryad* 1343, *Tyriage* 1390 'land of Eth' from Gaelic *tìr* 'land' and a specific element *Eth* which is unlikely to be Gaelic *ith* 'corn' as has been popularly suggested, and thus remains obscure. [*tie-**ree***]

Tobermory (Argyll & Bute) *Tibbermore* 1540 'St Mary's well' from Gaelic *tobar* 'well' and *Moire* 'the Virgin Mary'. [*toe-ber-**moar**-ee*]

Tomatin (Highland) *Tomatin* 1820 'juniper knoll' from Gaelic *tom* 'hill, knoll' and *aiteann* 'juniper'. [*to-**mat**-in*]

Tomich (Highland) *Tomach* 1655 'hillock place' from Gaelic *tom* 'hill, knoll' with an *–ach* suffix indicating 'place of'. [***tom**-ich*]

Tomintoul (Moray) *Tomantoul* 1820 'knoll of the barn' from Gaelic *tom* 'hill, knoll' *an t-* 'of the' *sabhail* (from *sabhal*) 'barn'. [*tom-in-**towl***]

Tomnahurich (Highland) *Toimnihurich* 1690 'knoll of the yew trees' from Gaelic *tom* 'hill, knoll' *na h-* 'of the' *iubhraich* 'yew trees'. [*tom-na-**hyoor**-ich*]

Tongue (Highland) *Toung* 1542 'tongue of land' from Old Norse *tunga* 'tongue, spit of land'. [***tung***]

Torridon (Highland) *Torvirtayne* 1464, *Torrerdone* 1584 'place of portage' from Gaelic *toirbheartan* 'place of transference', a term related to Gaelic *tairbeart* 'a portage'. [***torr**-i-din*]

Torrisdale (Argyll & Bute, Highland) *Glentoresdale* a.1251 (AB), *Thorisdaill* 1565 (H) 'Thorir's valley' from the Old Norse personal name *Thorir* (from *Thor*) and *dalr* 'valley'. [***torr**-iss-dail*]

Torthorwald (Dumfries & Galloway) *Torthorald* 1214–18 'Thorwald's hill' from Gaelic *torr* 'hill' and the Old Norse personal name *Þorvaldr*. [***toth**-or-ald*]

Toward (Argyll & Bute) *Toward* 1498 'promontory of the hollows' from Gaelic *toll* 'hole, hollow' and *àird, àrd* 'height, promontory'. [***tow**-ard*]

Trabroun (East Lothian) *Trabroun* 1516, **Trabrown** (Borders) *Treuerbrun* c.1170 'settlement of the hill' Brittonic *tref* 'farm, settlement' *yr* 'of the' *bryn* 'hill'. [*tra-**broon***]

Tranent (East Lothian) *Trauernent* c.1127, *Treuernent* 1144 'settlement of the stream(s)' from Brittonic *tref* 'farm, settlement' *yr* 'of the' *nant* 'stream, valley', perhaps in the plural form *neint*. [*tra-**nent***]

Traprain Law (East Lothian) *Trepprene* c.1370 'hill of the tree-farm' from Brittonic *tref* 'farm, settlement' and *pren* 'tree', to which Scots *law* 'rounded hill' was later added. [*tra-prain-**law***]

Traquair (Borders) *Trevequyrd* c.1124, *Treuequor* a.1153 'settlement of the River Quair' from Brittonic *tref* 'farm, settlement' *yr* 'of the' and the river name Quair, from Brittonic *Gweir*, earlier *Vedra* 'the clear one'. [*tra-**kwair***]

Troon (South Ayrshire) *Trone* 1371, *Trune* 1464 'the headland' from Brittonic *trwyn* 'headland, point'. [***troon***]

Trossachs (Stirling) 'the cross hills' In Gaelic the name is *Na Tròsaichean*, which may have been adapted from Brittonic *traws-fynydd* 'cross-hills'. The Anglicised version retains the plural form from the Gaelic name. [***tross**-aks*, ***tross**-achs*]

Trotternish (Highland) *Trouternesse, Tronternesse* 1549 'Thrond's headland' from the Old Norse personal name *Thrond* (in the possessive form *Throndar*) and *nes* 'headland'. [***trott**-er-neesh*]

Turnberry (South Ayrshire) *Tornebiri* 1214, *Turnberige* 1226 perhaps 'thorn fort' from Old English *þyrne* 'thorn' and *byrig*, the dative form of *burh* 'fortified place'. [***turn**-burr-ay*]

Turriff (Aberdeenshire) *Turbruaid* 10thC The modern Gaelic form is *Torraibh*, apparently meaning 'hill place' from *tòrr* 'hill, heap' with an *–aibh* dative plural ending. However the historical form reveals that this was not the orginal form of the name, which is now obscure. [***turr**-iff*]

Tweeddale (Borders) *Tweddal* 1147–50, *Twedall* 1360 'valley of the river Tweed' from an obscure Brittonic river-name and Old English *dæl* 'valley'. [***tweed**-dail*]

Twynholm (Dumfries & Galloway) *Twignam* 1154–65, *Twenham* 1200-06 either 'Twicga's homestead' from the Old English personal name *Twicga* and *hām* 'homestead, village', or '(place) between the streams' from Old English *(be)twēonan* 'between' and *ēam*, the dative plural form of *ēa* 'stream, river'. [***twine**-um*]

Tyndrum (Argyll & Bute) *Tyndrum* 1820 'house on the ridge' from Gaelic *taigh* 'house' *an* 'of the' *druim* 'ridge'. [***tyne**-drum*]

Tyninghame (East Lothian) *Tininghami* 756, *Tinnigaham* c.1050 'village of the settlers by the Tyne' from the river name *Tyne* and Old English *inga* 'of the settlers' and *hām* 'homestead, village'. [***tin**-ing-um*]

Uddingston (South Lanarkshire) *Odistoun* 1296 'Oda's farm' from the Old English personal name *Oda* and *tūn* 'village, farm, estate'. [***udd**-ing-stun*]

Uig (Highland, Western Isles) *Wig* 1512 (H), *Vye* 1549, *Vyg* c.1620 (WI) 'the bay' from Gaelic *ùig* 'bay', a loanword from Old Norse *vík* . [***oo**-ig*]

Uist (Western Isles) *Iuist* 1282, *Ywest* 1344, *Ouiste* 1373 This name is obscure. It has been interpreted as 'inner abode' from Old Norse *í* 'in' and *vist* 'dwelling', but it is likely that this is an older pre-Celtic name. [***yoo**-ist*, locally ***oo**-ist*]

Ulbster (Highland) *Ulbister* 1538 'Ulf's farm' from the Old Norse personal name *Ulfr* and *bólstaðr* 'dwelling, farmstead'. [***ulb**-ster*]

Ullapool (Highland) *Ullebell* 1592, *Ullabill* 1596 'farm of the wolves' from the plural of Old Norse *ulfr* 'wolf' and *bœli* 'farm'. [***ull**-a-pool*]

Urquhart (Highland) *Airchartdan* c.700 'woodside' from Pictish *ar* 'at, beside' and *carrden* 'thicket, copse'. [***urch**-urt*]

Watten (Highland) *Watne* c.1230 'the lake' from Old Norse *vatn* 'lake, water'. [***watt**-en*]

Weddersbie (Fife) *Wedderisbe* 1509 'wether farm' from Old Norse *veðr* 'wether, castrated ram' and and *bœr, býr* 'farm, settlement'. [***wed**-erz-bee*]

Wemyss (North Ayrshire, Fife) *Wemes* c.1180 (F) *Wemyss Bay* 1820 (NA) '(place of) caves' from Gaelic *uaimh* 'cave' and the Old Gaelic suffix *–es* which indicates 'place of'. [***weems***]

Westerkirk (Dumfries & Galloway) *Wadsterker* 1249 'Styrkarr's ford' from Old Norse *vað* 'ford' and the Old Norse personal name *Styrrkárr.* [***west**-er-kirk*]

West Kilbride (North Ayrshire) *Kilbryde* 1315–21, *West Kilbride* 1718 '(western) church of St Brigid' from Gaelic *cill* 'church' and one of the sixteen Celtic saints named *Brigid.* 'West' was added later to distinguish the town from East Kilbride in South Lanarkshire. [*west-kil-**bride***]

West Linton (Borders) *Lyntoun* 1567 '(western) flax farm' from Old English *līn* 'flax' and *tūn* 'village, farm, estate'. 'West' was added later to distinguish the town from East Linton in East Lothian. [*west-**lin**-tun*]

Whitburn (West Lothian) *Whiteburne* 1296 'white stream' from Old English *hwīt* 'white, clear' and *burna* 'stream'. [***whit**-burn*]

Whithorn (Dumfries & Galloway) *Huuitern* c.1100 'white house' from Old English *hwīt* 'white, clear' and *ærn* 'house, dwelling'. This is the famous white house or church of St Ninian, also known in the Latin form *Candida Casa* and the Gaelic form *Futarna.* [***whit**-horn*]

Wick (Highland) *Weke* 1478 'the bay' from Old Norse *vík* 'bay'. [***wick***]

Wigtown (Dumfries & Galloway) *Wiketune* 1232 'Wicga's farmstead' or 'dairy farmstead' from the Old English personal name *Wicga* or the word *wīc* '(dairy) farm, settlement', combined with *tūn* 'village, farm, estate'. [***wig**-tin*]

Wishaw (North Lanarkshire) *Wischaw* 1544 perhaps 'willow wood' or 'white wood' from Scots *withy, widdie* 'willow' or *whit, whyt* 'white' and *shaw* 'thicket, small wood'. [***wish**-awe*]

Hill Names

Am Bodach (Highland) 'the old man' from Gaelic *am* 'the' and *bodach* 'old man'. [*am-**bo**-toch*]

An Caisteal (Stirling) 'the castle' from Gaelic *an* 'the' and *caisteal* 'castle'. [*an-**kash**-*tyal]

An Riabhachan (Highland) 'the brindled one' from Gaelic *an* 'the' and *riabhach* 'brindled one, streaked one'. [*an-**ree**-a-voch-an*]

An Stùc (Perth & Kinross) 'the pinnacle' from Gaelic *an* 'the' and *stùc* 'pinnacle, little cliff'. [*an-**stoochk***]

An Teallach (Highland) 'the forge' from Gaelic *an* 'the' and *teallach* 'forge, hearth'. [*an-**tya**-lach*]

Aonach Eagach (Highland) 'jagged hill' from Gaelic *aonach* 'steep, ridged hill' and *eagach* 'jagged, notched'. [*oe-noch-**aig**-ach*]

Aonach Mor (Highland) 'the big (ridged) hill' from Gaelic *aonach* 'steep, ridged hill' and *mòr* 'large, great'. [*oe-noch-**moar***]

Beinn Alligin (Highland) perhaps 'jewel mountain' from Gaelic *beinn* 'mountain' and *àilleagan* 'a jewel, a darling'. [*bain-**aa**-li-ginn*]

Beinn Bhreac (various) 'speckled mountain' from Gaelic *beinn* 'mountain' and *bhreac* (from *breac*) 'speckled'. [*bain-**vrechk***]

Beinn Dearg (various) 'red mountain' from Gaelic *beinn* 'mountain' and *dearg* 'red'. [*bain-**jer**-ek*]

Beinn Dòrain (Argyll & Bute) either 'mountain of the streamlets' or 'otter mountain' from Gaelic *beinn* 'mountain' and either *dobharan* 'streamlets' or *dòbhran* 'otter'. [*bain-**doar**-an*]

Beinn Each (Stirling) 'horse mountain' from Gaelic *beinn* 'mountain' and *each* 'horse'. [*bain-**aich***]

Beinn Eighe (Highland) 'notch mountain' from Gaelic *beinn* 'mountain' and *eige* (from *eag*) 'notch, gap, file'. [*bain-**aiy***]

Beinn Ghlas (Perth & Kinross) 'grey-green mountain' from Gaelic *beinn* 'mountain' and *ghlas* (from *glas*) 'grey, green'. [*bain-**ghlas***]

Beinn Ìme (Argyll & Bute) 'butter mountain' from Gaelic *beinn* 'mountain' and *ìme* (from *ìm*) 'butter'. The name refers to the practise of keeping herds high on the mountainside and making butter at hill shielings. [*ben-**eem***]

Beinn Narnain (Argyll & Bute) probably 'mountain of notches' from Gaelic *beinn* 'mountain' and *bèarnan* 'notches, gaps'. [*ben-**nar**-nain*]

Beinn Odhar (Argyll & Bute) 'tawny mountain' from Gaelic *beinn* 'mountain' and *odhar* 'pale, dun, tawny'. [*ben-**oh**-ar*]

Ben Alder (Highland) 'mountain of the water of rock' from Gaelic *beinn* 'mountain' and *ail-dhobair*, a stream-name containing *ail* 'rock' and *dobhar* 'water, stream'. [*ben-**ol**-der*]

Ben Arthur or **The Cobbler** (Argyll & Bute) The Gaelic name is 'Arthur's mountain' from Gaelic *beinn* 'mountain' and *Artair*, the legendary British king. The name is recorded as *Suy Arthire* in the late sixteenth century, showing that *beinn* has replaced *suidhe* 'seat', in parallel with Arthur's Seat in Edinburgh. The English name originally referred only to the central peak, which was considered to resemble a cobbler hunched over his work. [*ben-**ar**-thur, the-**kob**ler*]

Ben Avon (Highland) probably 'mountain of the river' from Gaelic containing *beinn* 'mountain' and *abhainn* 'river'. The river Avon is nearby. [*ben-**aan***]

Ben Chonzie or **Ben-y-Hone** (Perth & Kinross) 'mossy mountain' from Gaelic *Beinn a' Chòinnich*, containing *beinn* 'mountain' *a'* 'the' and *còinnich* 'mossy'. [*ben-ee-**hoan**,* locally *ben-**hon**-zay*]

Ben Cleuch (Perth & Kinross) probably 'stony mountain' from Gaelic *beinn* 'mountain' and *cloich* (from *clach*) 'stone', rather than Scots *cleuch* 'ravine'. [*ben-**klooch***]

Ben Cruachan (Argyll & Bute) 'heap mountain' from Gaelic *beinn* 'mountain' and *cruachan* 'heap, stack'. [*ben-**kroo**-a-chan*]

Ben Hee (Highland) 'fairy mountain' from Gaelic *beinn* 'mountain' and *shìth* (from *sìth*) 'fairy (hill)'. [*ben-**hee***]

Ben Hope (Highland) 'mountain of the bay' from Gaelic *beinn* and Old Norse *hópr* 'landlocked bay, inlet'. The mountain takes its name from nearby Loch Hope. [*ben-**hoap***]

Ben Lawers (Perth & Kinross) 'mountain of the noisy stream' from Gaelic *beinn* 'mountain' and *labhar* 'loud, noisy (stream)'. [*ben-**law**-ers*]

Ben Lomond (Stirling) probably 'beacon mountain' from Gaelic *beinn* 'mountain' and Brittonic/Pictish *llumon* 'a beacon'. [*ben-**loa**-mond*]

Ben Lui (Stirling) 'calf mountain' from Gaelic *beinn* 'mountain' and *laoigh* (from *laogh*) 'calf'. [*ben-**loo**-ee*]

Ben Macdui (Moray) 'MacDuff's mountain' from Gaelic *beinn* 'mountain' and the Gaelic form of the surname *MacDuff*, which may be a reference to local landowners, the Earls of Fife. [*ben-mac-**doo**-ee*]

Ben More (various) 'great mountain' from Gaelic *beinn* 'mountain' and *mòr* 'large, great'. [b*en-**moar***]

Bennachie (Aberdeenshire) 'mountain of the breast(s)' from Gaelic *beinn* 'mountain' *na* 'of the' *cìche* (from *cìoch*) 'breast, nipple'. [*ben-a-**chee***]

Ben Nevis (Highland) This is a difficult name. It may be 'mountain of the river Nevis' from Gaelic *beinn* 'mountain' and the river-name *Nevis* from the pre-Celtic root **nebh-* 'moist, water, mist'. Alternatively, it may be 'venomous mountain' from *beinn* and *nimheis* 'venomous'. [*ben-**nev**-is*]

Ben Oss (Stirling) probably 'elk mountain' from Gaelic *beinn* 'mountain' and *os* 'stag, elk', although the second element could also be *òs* 'stream outlet'. [*ben-**oss***]

Ben Vane (Argyll & Bute) 'middle mountain' from Gaelic *beinn* 'mountain' and *mheadhoin* (from *meadhan*) 'middle'. [*ben-**vain***]

Ben Vorlich (Argyll & Bute, Perth & Kinross) 'mountain of the sack-shaped bay' from Gaelic *beinn* 'mountain' and *muir-bolg* (in the form *mhuir'lag*) literally a 'sea-bag', usually applied to a rounded sea-inlet. [*ben-**vor**-lich*]

Ben Vuirich (Perth & Kinross) 'mountain of the roaring' from Gaelic *beinn* 'mountain' and *bhùirich* (from *bùirich*) 'roaring', a reference to the noise made by the rutting stags. [*ben-**voor**-ich*]

Ben Wyvis (Highland) perhaps 'awesome mountain' from Gaelic *beinn* 'mountain' and *uamhas* 'awesome, atrocious, enormous'. [*ben-**wiv**-is,* locally *ben-**wee**-vis*]

Braeriach or **Am Bràigh Riabhach** (Moray) 'the brindled upland' from Gaelic *am* 'the' *bràigh* 'upland, upper part' and *riabhach* 'brindled, streaky, grey'. [*bray-**ree**-ach,* locally *bry-**ree**-ach*]

Buachaille Etive Mòr and **Buachaille Etive Beag** (Argyll & Bute) These two mountains are 'the big herdsman of Etive' and 'the little herdsman of Etive' respectively, from Gaelic *buachaille* 'herdsman, shepherd' and the place-name *Etive* together with *beag* 'small' and *mòr* 'large, great'. [***boo**-ach-ill-et-iv-**moar**, **boo**-ach-ill-et-iv-**bek***]

Cairn Gorm (Highland) 'blue rocky peak' from Gaelic *càrn* 'heap of stones, rocky peak' and *gorm* 'blue'. The 'Cairngorms' take their name from this mountain. [*cairn-**gorm***]

Cairn Toul or **Càrn an t-Sabhail** (Moray) 'rocky peak of the barn' from Gaelic *càrn* 'heap of stones, rocky peak' knoll' *an t-* 'of the' *sabhail* (from *sabhal*) 'barn'. The name may refer to the barn-like shape of the mountain. [*cairn-**tool***]

Cairnwell (Aberdeenshire) 'the rocky peak of the bags' from Gaelic *càrn* 'heap of stones, rocky peak' and *bhalg* (from *balg*) 'bag'. [***cairn**-well*]

Càrn Aosda (Aberdeenshire) perhaps 'ancient rocky peak' from Gaelic *càrn* 'heap of stones, rocky peak' and *aosda* 'aged, ancient'. [*caarn-**oas**-ta*]

Càrn Eige (Highland) 'notched rocky peaky' from Gaelic *càrn* 'heap of stones, rocky peak' and *eige* (from *eag*) 'notch, gap, file'. [*caarn-**aik**-yeh*]

Càrn Mòr Dearg (Highland) 'great red rocky peak' from Gaelic *càrn* 'heap of stones, rocky peak' *mòr* 'large, great' and *dearg* 'red'. [*caarn-moar-**jer**-ek*]

Càrn nan Gobhar (Highland) 'rocky peak of the goat(s)' from Gaelic *càrn* 'heap of stones, rocky peak' *nan* 'of the' *gobhar* 'goat'. [*caarn-nan-**gow**-er*]

Cùl Beag and **Cùl Mòr** (Highland) These two mountains mean 'little back' and 'big back' respectively, from Gaelic *cùl* 'back' together with *beag* 'small' and *mòr* 'large, great'. [*cool-**bek**, cool-**moar***]

Garbh Bheinn (various) 'rough mountain' from Gaelic *garbh* 'rough, coarse' and *bheinn* (from *beinn*) 'mountain'. [***gar**-av-vain*]

Goat Fell (North Ayrshire) 'hill of the goats' from Old Norse *geitar* 'goats' and *fjall* 'hill, mountain'. [*goat-**fell***]

Lochnagar (Aberdeenshire) 'noisy little loch' from Gaelic *lochan* 'small loch' *na* 'of the' *gàire* 'noise, laughter'. This mountain takes its name from the nearby loch *Lochan na Gàire*, but was originally known as *Beinn nan Cìochan* 'mountain of the breasts'. [*loch-na-**gar***]

Màm Sodhail (Highland) properly **Màm Sabhail** 'rounded hill of the barn' from Gaelic *màm* 'breast, rounded hill, pass' and *sabhail* (from *sabhal*) 'barn'. [*maam-**sool***]

Meall Buidhe (various) 'yellow hill' from Gaelic *meall* 'round hill, a lump' and *buidhe* 'yellow'. [*myowl-**boo**-yeh*]

Meall Garbh (various) 'rough hill' from Gaelic *meall* 'round hill, a lump' and *garbh* 'rough, coarse'. [*myowl-**gar**-av*]

Meall Odhar (Perth & Kinross) 'tawny hill' from Gaelic *meall* 'round hill, a lump' and *odhar* 'pale, dun, tawny'. [*myowl-**oa**-ur*]

Meall nan Tàrmachan (Perth & Kinross) 'hill of the ptarmigans' from Gaelic *meall* 'round hill, a lump' *nan* 'of the' *tàrmachan* 'ptarmigan'. [*myowl-nan-**taar**-moch-an*]

Merrick (the) (Dumfries & Galloway) 'pronged (hill)' from Gaelic *meurach* 'pronged, branched, fingered'. [*the-**merr**-ick*]

Morven (Aberdeenshire, Highland) 'big mountain' from Gaelic *mòr* 'large, great' and *bheinn* (from *beinn*) 'mountain'. [***mor**-ven*]

Mount Keen (Aberdeenshire) 'gentle mountain' from Gaelic *monadh* 'mountain' and *caoin* 'gentle'. [*mount-**keen***]

Quinag (Highland) 'the milk-pail' from Gaelic *cuinneag* 'milk-pail, churn', which is probably a reference to the shape of the hill. [***koon**-yak*]

Ruadh Stac Mor (Highland) 'big red stack' from Gaelic *ruadh* 'red, brown' *stac* 'stack, precipice' and *mòr* 'large, great'. [*roo-agh-stachk-**moar***]

Scaraben (Highland) 'notched mountain' from Old Norse *skora* 'notch, incision' and Gaelic *beinn* 'mountain' which may have replaced an original Norse element such as *fjall* 'hill, mountain'. [***scar**-a-ben*]

Schiehallion (Perth & Kinross) 'fairy hill of the Caledonians' from Gaelic *sìth* 'fairy (hill)' and *Chailleann* 'Caledonians'. [*shee-**hal**-yan*]

Sgùrr Alasdair (Highland) 'Alasdair's peak' from Gaelic *sgùrr* 'pointed hill, peak' and the name of Sheriff Alexander Nicolson (*Alasdair MacNeacail*) of Skye who made the first recorded ascent of the mountain in 1873. [*skoor-**al**-as-tar*]

Sgùrr Bàn (Highland) 'pale peak' from Gaelic *sgùrr* 'pointed hill, peak' and *bàn* 'fair, pale, white, light'. [*skoor-**baan***]

Sgùrr na Lapaich (Highland) 'peak of the bogland' from Gaelic *sgùrr* 'pointed hill, peak' *na* 'of the' *lapaich* 'bogland'. [*skoor-na-**lap**-ich*]

Sgùrr nan Gillean (Highland) although the modern form suggests 'peak of the young men' from Gaelic *sgùrr* 'pointed hill, peak' *nan* 'of the', *gillean* 'young men' (from *gille* 'boy, lad'), this is more probably 'peak of gullies' from *gilean* 'gullies' which derives from *gil*, an Old Norse loanword into Gaelic meaning 'ravine, gully'. [*skoor-nan-**geel**-yan*]

Sròn Garbh (various) 'rough point' from Gaelic *sròn* 'nose, point, promontory' and *garbh* 'rough, coarse'. [*strawn-**gar**-av*]

Stac Pollaidh (Highland) 'stack of the river Pollaidh' from Gaelic *stac* 'stack, precipice' and the river *Pollaidh* derived from *poll* 'pool, hollow'. [*stack-**poll**-ee*]

Stob Coire nan Lochan (Argyll & Bute) 'peak of the corrie of the little loch(s)' from Gaelic *stob* 'steep hill, peak, point' *coire* 'corrie, hollow' *nan* 'of the' *lochan* '(small) loch'. [*stop-kor-a-nan-**loch**-an*]

Stob Dubh (Argyll & Bute) 'black peak' from Gaelic *stob* 'steep hill, peak, point' and *dubh* 'black'. [*stop-**doo***]

Stob Ghabhar (Highland) 'goat peak' from Gaelic *stob* 'steep hill, peak, point' and *ghabhar* (from *gobhar*) 'goat'. [*stop-**ghow**-er*]

Stùc a' Chròin (Perth & Kinross) probably 'peak of the little sheepfold' from Gaelic *stùc* 'peak, pinnacle' *a'* 'of the' *cròthan* 'little sheepfold'. [*stoochk-a-**chroyn***]

Suilven (Highland) 'pillar mountain' from Old Norse *súl* 'pillar and Gaelic *beinn* 'mountain', which may have replaced an original Norse element such as *fjall* 'hill, mountain'. [***sool**-ven*]

Further Information

Names

George F. Black, *The Surnames of Scotland: Their Origin, Meaning and History* (1946, reprinted 1999)
Ian Fraser, *The Place-Names of Arran* (1999)
Roddy Maclean, *The Gaelic Place Names and Heritage of Inverness* (2004)
A. D. Mills, *A Dictionary of British Place Names* (2003)
W. F. H. Nicolaisen, *The Picts and Their Place Names* (1996)
W. F. H. Nicolaisen, *Scottish Place-Names*, New Edition (2001)
Maggie Scott, *Scottish Place Names* (2008)
Simon Taylor, *The Place-Names of Fife*, 2 volumes so far (2006, 2008)
W. J. Watson, *The History of the Celtic Place-Names of Scotland* (1926, reprinted 1993)
W. J. Watson, *Place-Names of Ross and Cromarty* (1924, reprinted 1996)
W. J. Watson, *Scottish Place-Name Papers* (2002)

The Languages of Scotland

Edward Dwelly, *The Illustrated Gaelic-English Dictionary* (1911, reprinted 1993)
Iseabail Macleod, *The Pocket Guide to Scottish Words* (2006)
Iseabail Macleod *et al*, *The Scots Thesaurus* (1990)
Mairi Robinson *et al*, *The Concise Scots Dictionary* (1985)

Hill Names

Peter Drummond, *Scottish Hill Names: Their Origin and Meaning* (2007)
Derek A. Bearhop *et al*, *Munro's Tables and Other Tables of Lower Hills* (1997)

Websites

www.spns.org.uk
The Scottish Place-Name Society was established in 1996, and their website contains summaries of conference papers, toponymic databases and useful information on further reading and resources.

www.ordnancesurvey.co.uk/oswebsite/freefun/didyouknow/placenames
The place-name section of Ordnance Survey website contains useful introductory material on Gaelic, Scandinavian, Scots and Welsh place-names including guides to grammar and pronunciation, together with comprehensive lists of the most common elements.

www.dsl.ac.uk
The Dictionary of the Scots Language website combines the twelve-volume *Dictionary of the Older Scottish Tongue* and the ten-volume *Scottish National Dictionary* in a fully searchable format.